Praise for *How to Be a High School Superstar*

"Disguised as a peppy college-admission guide, Newport's book is actually a profound, life-affirming manifesto for ambitious high school students. Forgo the sleepless and cynical path to college acceptance. Instead, blaze your trail to the Ivy League by living a full life and immersing yourself in things that matter. Relax. Find meaning. Be you."

—David Shenk, author of *The Genius in All of Us*

"*How to Be a High School Superstar* should be on the shelf of every student who wonders how to stand out in the increasingly competitive race to get into a top college. Cal Newport has a keen sense of what types of students and activities appeal to college admissions officers, and his advice is exceptionally easy to execute. His approach will not only help you win the admissions race, it will keep you sane while you run the marathon."

—Joie Jager-Hyman, author of *Fat Envelope Frenzy* and
B+ Grades, A+college Application

"This book changes everything. Put away your traditional college plan and get ready to learn something that really works."

—Chris Guillebeau, author of *The $100 Startup* and
The Art of Non-Conformity

How to Be a High School Superstar

A Revolutionary Plan to Get into College
by Standing Out (Without Burning Out)

Cal Newport

THREE RIVERS PRESS
NEW YORK

To Julie

Copyright © 2010 by Calvin C. Newport

All rights reserved.
Published in the United States by Three Rivers Press,
an imprint of the Crown Publishing Group,
a division of Random House, Inc., New York.
www.crownpublishing.com

THREE RIVERS PRESS and the Tugboat design are trademarks of
Random House, Inc.

Originally published in the United States by Broadway Books, and imprint of
the Crown Publishing Group, a division of Random House, Inc., New York,
in 2010.

Library of Congress Cataloging-in-Publication Data
Newport, Cal.
   How to be a high school superstar : a revolutionary plan to get into college
by standing out (without burning out) / by Cal Newport.
      p. cm.
   1. Universities and colleges—United States—Admission. 2. College
choice—United States. I. Title.
   LB2351.2.N5 2010
   378.1'610973—dc22   2009046623

ISBN 978-0-7679-3258-5

Printed in the United States of America

Design by Ruth Lee-Mui

16 15 14 13 12 11 10

First Edition

Contents

A NOTE FOR PARENTS

This book is written for high school students. You'll notice throughout that I directly address the student concerning his or her journey
through high school and the admissions process. I highly recommend, however, that parents read the book as well. The strategies
described in the chapters that follow work best if the entire household
is involved.

Introduction:
"Stanford Doesn't Take Students with Bs!"

IN LATE spring 2004, a nervous student walked through the doors of the college counseling center at an elite Bay Area private high school. The student, whom I'll call Kara, had an appointment to discuss her college prospects. She entered a cramped office. The space was dominated by a desk, and what little area remained was taken up by a small round table. Multiracial clusters of happy students beamed at her from the college brochures pinned to the wall.

Kara took a seat at the table. Across from her sat her college counselor, a redheaded woman, pregnant and in her late twenties, flipping through a file. Kara thought she saw concern flash across the counselor's face.

After the obligatory small talk, the counselor began the session. "So, how are your grades going to be this semester?" she asked.

"Not as good as I hoped, probably some Bs," Kara answered.

The counselor glanced down at the list of schools where Kara wanted to apply, as if reconfirming, for the umpteenth time, that she had read it right. "Stanford has a ten percent acceptance rate. Do you know what that means?" she asked.

"That one out of ten get in?" Kara ventured.

"It means that nine get rejected," the counselor replied, trying to keep her voice even and reassuring. She paused for a moment, then asked, "Kara, do you think that you're better than those nine other people?"

Kara began to stammer a response.

"Kara," the counselor said pleadingly, "Stanford doesn't take students with Bs." She pulled a sheet from the folder. "You're on the cross-country team, which is good. But you're not the president of any clubs, and with these mediocre grades you're not going to get into your reach schools. You're just not. The people who apply to these schools have done *amazing* things."

Though it was left unsaid, Kara knew exactly the type of "amazing" student her counselor meant—students like Elizabeth, who was Kara's best friend and one of the high school's most impressive seniors. Elizabeth was a master at the college admissions game, someone Kara later described to me as "the poster child for students who do lots of uninteresting things." Elizabeth was president of the key club, played piano and varsity tennis, competed in math competitions, and belonged to what Kara described as "lots of boring clubs that I would never join."

When it came to grades, nothing short of straight As would satisfy Elizabeth. She was maniacal about gaming courses, figuring out which would consistently yield As in exchange for hard work and avoiding those that relied too much on insight or natural ability (attributes that scared her off because they could not be acquired by raw effort). Like many students at her high school, she suffered from what Kara called "gratuitous AP taking." By contrast, Kara, much to the horror of her counselor, had only taken three advanced placement courses. Keep in mind that her school had practically coronated a student who had broken the state record for the most APs taken by a freshman.

In the first few weeks of that spring semester, Elizabeth had dropped a course because she got a B on the first test, which increased the risk of her missing a full A for her final grade. She then pleaded with Kara to drop a linear algebra course that was giving her trouble. "Take AP stats instead," she said. "All you have to do is a crapload of homework—that's forty percent of the grade; if you do it all they give you an A." Kara ignored this advice. She liked linear algebra.

Elizabeth, on the other hand, didn't like much at all about high school. As Kara recalls: "Elizabeth was working all the time; she had no social life; she was just so freakin' diligent!" She was also, as you might imagine, stress-addled and often upset or anxious. But this is the approach that most students at her elite high school swore by. It's also the approach followed by tens of thousands of other talented but overworked students across the country. It persists for one simple reason: if you're not an amazing athlete or a genius, and if your parents aren't capable of donating a new library to Harvard, demonstrating time-consuming "commitment" to lots of things has been deemed the only reliable way to maximize your admissions chances. It's a brutal game, and it's no fun to play, but at least the rules are clear.

Then along came Kara.

Spooked by the grim encounter with her college counselor—a meeting that concluded with the counselor pulling out the applications for the less-competitive California public universities—Kara scraped together enough money to apply to twenty-one different schools. (Her dad refused to pay that many application fees.)

"I was freaked out that I wasn't going to get in anywhere," she recalls.

But here's the thing: Kara did get in. In fact, she got into twenty of the twenty-one schools she applied to, including MIT, Caltech, Columbia, Cornell, Berkeley, Johns Hopkins, and, of course, Stanford—proving, to the surprise of her counselor, that those schools do occasionally accept students with Bs.

Kara's long string of acceptances surprised her classmates because she had refused to play the standard admissions game. Kara had the lowest GPA of any student from her school who had ever been accepted into MIT (where she now attends). She took a reasonable course load and avoided a crushing extracurricular schedule. Unlike most of her competitive peers, Kara actually enjoyed high school.

"I was perceived as the relaxed kid in my school," she told me with a sheepish grin. It was as if she were admitting a crime.

As you might imagine, Kara's success proved disruptive. The entire motivation—the raison d'être—for the brutal schedules of students like Elizabeth is their unshakable confidence that doing more things than the thousands of other applicants applying to the same schools is the *only* way to stand out. Kara shattered this confidence, and in doing so she provided a glimmer of hope for stressed students everywhere: it might be possible to stand out without burning out.

Meet the Relaxed Superstars

Kara is part of a little-known subculture of students that I call the *relaxed superstars*. These are students who live relaxed and happy high school lives yet still breeze into their reach schools. Like Kara, they challenge a lot of what we thought was true about the college admissions process.

Most relaxed superstars pay little attention to college admissions until application deadlines loom—the topic doesn't dominate their lives the way it does for so many of their peers. They dismiss the belief that you should suffer through the hardest possible course schedules; instead, they build reasonable schedules that provide challenge but still leave plenty of free time. They abhor crowded lists of extracurricular activities; instead, they focus on a small number of genuinely interesting pursuits.

Perhaps the most striking trait of these students is their happiness. Spending time with them, I have been astonished by how much they seemed to enjoy their lives. They flat-out reject the idea that happiness must be deferred until after you get accepted into college, and they prove that living a relaxed and engaging life can actually make you *more* successful in the admissions process.

This book presents the first insider look into the fascinating world of these students. For the past three years, I've tracked down relaxed superstars from across the country and listened to their stories. During my research I met Olivia, for example, a student from New Hampshire who earned a full-ride scholarship to the University of Virginia even though she spent, on average, only six or seven hours *per week* on extracurriculars during the school year. I also met Michael, from Paradise Valley, Arizona, who took only one AP course during the dreaded junior year and dedicated his abundant free time to a single activity. Most impressive to me was the fact that during the school week, at least four days out of five, Michael would set off, after the final bell, on a trail that cut through campus before winding its way to the summit of a nearby desert mountain. The hike took from one to two hours, depending on which route he chose. At the top, sitting among the scrub grass and sweating in the dry Arizona heat, Michael would clear his head.

"When I would start up the mountain, I might have something bothering me," he said. "By the time I came down, it was not as big as it had seemed."

It's hard to find a happier or more well-balanced high school student. This Zen senior was accepted at Stanford.

I also met Maneesh, who described himself as "the laziest student at Bella Vista High School"—a large public school tucked away in a Northern California suburb. Maneesh somehow rigged his senior year schedule so that he could leave school at 11 a.m.

every day. When I asked him what he did with this free time, he laughed before replying, "Dude, whatever I wanted."

He was serious. He used the time in random ways, notably in figuring out how to build a cheap iPod case from an athletic sock—an idea that became an Internet sensation after he posted the plans online. Like Michael, Maneesh got into Stanford.

Maneesh was not the only relaxed superstar to rig an abbreviated school day. Another student, Kate, arranged her senior year school day to end before lunch so that she could work on an independent study project. Like Maneesh, she carried a light course load; she could often finish her daily homework by early afternoon. This, along with avoiding nearly all extracurricular activity beyond her independent study, made for a relaxed lifestyle. She got into Princeton while many of her friends—who had taken many more courses, scored better grades, and suffered through many more difficult extracurriculars—had to settle for the waitlist.

My inspiration for this project stems partly from the fact that I can count myself among the ranks of the relaxed superstars. As a member of the class of 2000 at a small central New Jersey public high school, I was infamous for my aversion to hard work. I never pulled an all-nighter and rarely worked past dinner. I scored mainly As, but Bs were sprinkled throughout my transcript, and there was even a C+ from a French class that never quite agreed with me.* I took AP courses, but never more than two or three at once, and I was a fan of study halls. In terms of formal extracurricular activities, I was my class's liaison, a member of the model UN club, and ran track—hardly an overwhelming load. As my good friend Michael Simmons recently

---

* As fans of my book *How to Become a Straight-A Student* know, it wasn't until college that I figured out the type of smart study habits that make it possible to combine a relaxed schedule with top grades.

admitted: "I was always amazed by how much time you seemed to spend relaxing."

When it came time for college admissions, I applied early to Dartmouth because I liked the students I had met during a whirl-wind tour of East Coast campuses. A few months later I received the acceptance notice. All told, the admissions process required only a few days of effort; it was never a major part of my student life.

Olivia, Michael, Maneesh, Kate, and I are just a few examples from among the many relaxed superstars you'll encounter in this book. Every story is true, though in some cases I've changed the student's name at his or her request. In the chapters that fol-low, you'll learn exactly how these stars pulled off their amazing combination of relaxation and admissions success. I'll then teach you how to replicate their feats in your own student life. Forget the stress and anxiety of the Elizabeth approach to college admis-sions. As the story of Kara suggests, you're about to learn a much better way.

Cracking the Superstar Code

At a high level of description, the secret to the relaxed superstars' success is straightforward: these students are *genuinely interest-ing people* who did *genuinely interesting things*. Kara, for example, developed a technology-based health curriculum. Olivia spent her summers working on horseshoe crab research at a nearby university. Michael spearheaded a series of sustainability projects at his school that earned considerable press attention. Maneesh wrote a bestselling guide to computer game programming for teens. Kate's research on teaching methods changed the way that a well-known charter school taught reading to its students. And I cofounded a Web development company.

As you'll learn, however, none of these accomplishments required an unusually large amount of work or a rare natural talent. In fact, I would argue that every one of these projects required less time than a varsity sport and less natural talent than that possessed by the violin players who sit in the first section of the school orchestra. When you combine this reality with the fact that these students took reasonable course loads and didn't add unrelated extracurriculars to their schedules, the observation that they lived relaxed and happy lives comes as no surprise. To an admissions officer, however, such students are superstars. Admissions officers are bored by applicants, like Elizabeth, who attempt to impress them through the sheer volume and difficulty of their accomplishments. They see right through faux passions carefully chosen to highlight aspects of the applicant's invented "personality." By contrast, students like Kara, Olivia, Michael, Maneesh, and Kate, who are genuinely interesting and doing genuinely interesting things, sparkle—even though their lives are much less stressful than those of the applicants they're outshining.

This high-level explanation, however, is not enough. Becoming genuinely interesting is not an easy task. After first hearing about relaxed superstars like those described above, the typical high school student will quickly survey his or her own life before declaring, "I have nothing that I'm that passionate about," and will then return to the cold comfort of the show-commitment-to-lots-of-different-activities strategy.

"The devil I know," the student thinks, "is better than the angel I don't understand."

Don't worry, the high-level explanation is just the beginning. This book moves beyond what these students did to get accepted and explains how they got started down their paths. In the chapters that follow, I deconstruct the lifestyle of the relaxed superstars, and then highlight the key ideas that will enable you to emulate their approach. Put another way, this book does not describe tricks for making you look more impressive. It provides, instead, advice for changing your life into one that naturally attracts impressive opportunities.

The Three Laws of the Relaxed Superstar

As my research into the relaxed superstars progressed, I began to notice three big-picture ideas popping up again and again:

The Law of Underscheduling
Pack your schedule with free time. Use this time to explore.

The Law of Focus
Master one serious interest. Don't waste time on unrelated activities.

The Law of Innovation
Pursue accomplishments that are hard to explain, not hard to do.

These were the general *laws* that most of the students I interviewed seemed to follow on their path from average to standout. This book is divided into three parts, one for each of these laws. Each part is then split into halves. The first half explains the law and gives examples of real relaxed superstars putting it into practice. The second half provides a *playbook* of specific advice to help you make the law an important part of your own life. By the time you finish all three parts, you'll have gained both a detailed understanding of the relaxed superstar lifestyle and a set of specific steps that can help you transform your own lifestyle to match.

The relaxed superstar philosophy is radical. If you're a student, I'm asking you to abandon much of the well-worn conventional wisdom about what you "must" do to get accepted into competitive colleges, and I'm offering you, instead, the hope that you can actually enjoy your high school life without sacrificing your long-term ambitions. If you're the parent of a student, I'm offering you the hope that your child can fulfill his or her potential without burning out or transforming into an unhappy, work-obsessed drone.

Along with these hopes, however, comes a request for your trust that the counterintuitive ideas I offer can actually work. With this in mind, I have provided, in the following section, the answers to some common questions about the relaxed superstar philosophy. I ask that you take a moment to skim these questions and answers to see if I address any objections or concerns you may have at this point.

By the time you finish this book, I hope you'll be a believer in the powerful idea that stress and admissions success are not inextricably linked. I've spent time with dozens of students who have proven that connection false. You're about to encounter many of their stories, and hopefully you'll join the growing ranks of relaxed superstars who've discovered, to their happy surprise, that college admissions doesn't have to be an ordeal to survive. Instead, as you will see, it can be a stress-free reward for living a happy, interesting life.

Common Questions About
the Relaxed Superstar Philosophy

Normal students can't write bestselling books or conduct breakthrough research, no matter how hard they try. These "relaxed superstars" sound like geniuses. How can you expect us mere mortals to replicate their amazing feats?

This is probably the most common reaction to the relaxed superstars. It is true that by the time these students apply to college, they're different from their peers. Among other things, they're surprisingly mature and engaged with the world. They also possess a knack for conceiving, and then pushing to completion, interesting projects. When you meet a relaxed superstar at this late stage, it does seem as if he or she possesses something special. **What's important to note, however, is that such students were not born with these abilities.** The traits that we admire developed as a side effect of their unique lifestyle—a lifestyle built around the three laws I describe in this book. This is the core idea of the relaxed superstar philosophy: **Genuinely interesting accomplishments are generated only by living a genuinely interesting life—not by special abilities or careful planning.**

This book provides a road map for constructing such a life.

It asks that you don't focus on the final accomplishments that made these students stars, but that you look instead at the path that led them to the place where such accomplishments come naturally.

How important are my grades and SAT scores if I follow the relaxed superstar lifestyle?

This is a crucial question that demands a clear answer: **Your grades and SAT scores together remain the most important factor in college admissions, even if you do follow the relaxed superstar lifestyle.** Most college guides will provide statistics on the median GPA and SAT scores of their accepted students. They typically describe a range of scores. For example, a school might report that the middle 50 percent of their accepted students scored between 650 and 700 on the math section of the SAT. This means that 25 percent of their accepted students scored above 700, 25 percent of these students scored below 650, and the rest scored somewhere in between. You can use these ranges to estimate your chance of being admitted. Here's my general rule: If your scores fall into the range of the top 25 percent of accepted students, then you can consider this school a *target*. With the exception of a handful of top universities, the school will probably accept you if you apply. If your score falls comfortably in the middle 50 percent, you can consider this school a *realistic reach*. You've passed the academic threshold for proof that you can handle the workload, but it's up to the other parts of your application to earn you a spot in the incoming class. If your scores are in the bottom 25 percent, then this school is probably out of your reach—regardless of your nonacademic achievements. Of course, exceptions abound, as any number of special circumstances can boost your chances—for example, if you're a recruited athlete or your parent is a senator—but this general rule applies to the majority of applicants.

With these terms defined, we can return to the original question and provide a more precise answer: **The relaxed superstar lifestyle will help you get accepted into your *realistic reach* schools.** It cannot guarantee that you will get into your *dream* school. If your grades and scores don't pass the minimum threshold, you're probably out of luck.

Keep in mind that, for some colleges, this threshold can be daunting. Consider Harvard. The middle 50 percent of its accepted students in the fall of 2008 had an SAT math score between 700 and 780. It follows that if you can't easily score in the 700 range on this section, then Harvard is likely off the table—regardless of your extracurricular prowess. At the same time, however, the relaxed superstar philosophy prevents you from needing to score a 790 or 800 to get in. Simply passing the middle 50 percent threshold is enough to allow the other aspects of your application to take over. This frees you from stressing out about getting the *highest* possible scores and grades. If you subscribe to the relaxed superstar philosophy, it's okay to have scores and grades that are *high enough*.

Can this book answer my technical questions about the college application process?

No. This book doesn't address the technical details of applying to colleges. I don't discuss the advantages of early decision, or provide a timeline for taking standardized tests. There are dozens of great guides—many of them written by college counselors or former admissions officers—that cover these technical details in depth. This book, by contrast, focuses exclusively on the one topic that these other titles miss: how to become the type of student who breezes through the admissions process.

I just finished my junior year of high school. Is it too late for me to reap the benefits of the relaxed superstar lifestyle?

There's no hard cutoff date after which these changes stop helping. Some of the students you'll encounter in this book, for example, made their transition to this lifestyle near the end of their junior year. The accomplishments that helped them stand out were completed in the fall of their senior year, right before applications were due. Other students, like Michael, the sustainability guru from Arizona, sent additional information to the colleges in the early spring of their senior year, after their applications were already submitted. (For a student on a waitlist, accomplishments from this final spring can make a difference, if brought to the attention of the admissions staff.)

That being said, the earlier you transform to the relaxed superstar lifestyle, the better. For one thing, it gives you more time to add interesting accomplishments. More important, each year you fail to live as a relaxed superstar is another year potentially marred by the stress and unhappiness that the traditional approach to college admissions generates.

Kids are too stressed out about college admissions. Shouldn't you be teaching the lesson that "there's more to life than Harvard" instead of focusing on "tricks" to beat the system?
Though it may be true that there's more to life than Harvard, the kids who are suffering the most from admissions-related stress are also the kids most likely to ignore this advice. This point was emphasized for me when I heard the following true story:

In the fall of 2007, Palo Alto's Gunn High School held an assembly led by Denise Pope, a Stanford researcher who specializes in high school stress. Gunn was an appropriate venue for this assembly, as the school is notorious for college-admissions-related anxiety. As Noreen Likins, the principal of Gunn High School, once commented about those of her students who were ailing: "When it spills over to kids getting two or three hours of sleep a night and doing too much, that's when we need to say enough is enough."

During the assembly, Pope highlighted the dangers of stress and outlined some alternative paths through college admissions—paths that emphasized finding a good fit over focusing exclusively on the most competitive schools.

"The students' reaction [to the assembly] was mixed," was the charitable summary included in a report published by the school later that year. The students were more candid. In an online discussion group, one Gunn junior sarcastically responded:

> Well, that assembly taught me that if I want to relieve my stress I should throw away all my college prospects . . . and go to some random Cal State University! Thank you, Gunn Administration, for letting us hear from the best in the field!

Later that year, a group of parents gathered at nearby Palo Alto High School's theater to attend a talk titled "Let's REALLY Talk About College." Originally billed as a "panel discussion for parents and students," the event had generated a buzz once it was revealed that several college admissions experts would sit on the panel.

Only a few minutes into the first speaker's presentation, however, it become clear that the focus of this assembly, as with Pope's talk, was the idea that students should look beyond the Ivy League and settle for less-competitive schools that would generate less stress. A murmur spread through the crowd. Someone stood up and walked out of the auditorium. More followed. As Louise Singleton, a college counselor who helped organize the event, estimates, at least 20 percent of the audience left before the first speaker finished.

I asked Louise why parents were ignoring this message, even though it was aimed at improving their kids' health.

"They think it's other people's problem," she told me. "They think, 'Not my kids—my kids will be okay.'"

The relaxed superstar lifestyle is the first admissions strategy that couples stress reduction with an improvement in your admissions chances. It allows students (and parents) who are wedded to the idea of getting into the best possible college to still have a shot at living a happy and relaxed life. With this in mind, this book doesn't contain tricks for beating the system. Instead, it focuses on building the type of sustainable lifestyle that can yield rewards not just in the admissions process, but also for life beyond.

Part 1

The Law of Underscheduling

Pack your schedule with free time. Use this time to explore.

The standard strategy for college admissions requires you to fill your schedule with as many activities as possible—and demonstrate a "passionate commitment" to each. The law of underscheduling discards this advice. In its place, it promotes the idea that your schedule should contain free time—*lots* of free time. But that's not all. You can't just use this free time to vegetate; you must fill it with unstructured exploration. That is, seek out things that seem interesting to you at the moment, and then follow up on whatever captures your attention most.

This lifestyle is exponentially more entertaining than one dominated by formal activities. But as you'll learn, it's also the secret to transforming yourself from a generic, bored, semi-articulate teen into someone genuinely interesting—one of the most important traits wielded by the relaxed superstars to succeed in admissions. Underscheduling provides the foundation for the lifestyle you're trying to build, so pay attention. Your life is about to seriously change.

In the chapters that follow, you'll meet Olivia and Jessica, two students who lived remarkably underscheduled lives yet still got into their dream schools. I'll use their stories to guide you through an exploration of exactly why the law of underscheduling works so well. Along the way, I'll banish the word "passion" from your vocabulary (replacing it with something much more precise), introduce you to some surprising research on how students become interesting, and challenge your assumptions about how much time is required to transform from average to fascinating. Part 1 ends with the longest and most detailed of the three playbooks presented in this book. This is no accident—successfully transitioning to an underscheduled lifestyle is the foundation of the relaxed superstar philosophy. The playbook provides specific advice for making underscheduling a reality in your own student life.

1

Horseshoe Crabs and Blogs

THE IDEA of drastically reducing your schedule probably sounds great in theory—who wouldn't want to enjoy an abundance of free time? But if you're like many students I've advised, you probably have reservations about the impact of such a lifestyle on your chances of getting into college. Running through the back of your mind is a simple logic: doing more is more impressive; therefore, by cutting back you're reducing your impressiveness, and this will hurt your admissions chances.

You will soon come to understand that this is a flawed belief. The number and difficulty of your accomplishments play only a minor role in college applications. Other factors are much more important.

Below, I introduce two students. The first, Olivia, dedicated only a handful of hours each week during the school year to extracurricular activities, yet still won a full-ride scholarship to the University of Virginia. The second, Jessica, was often able to finish her week's homework by Tuesday night—leaving the rest of the week free. She got accepted into the University of California, Berkeley, her dream school.

Their stories will help acclimate you to the concept that light schedules *can* correspond with admissions success. In the chapters that follow, we'll dive into the details of exactly why this is true and how you can replicate these results.

The Horseshoe Crab Effect

In late March of 2008, Olivia, a high school senior from a small town near Portsmouth, New Hampshire, was ushered into a room. She took a seat across from a semicircle of five distinguished-looking men and women. The group greeted her with wide smiles, but their eyes were serious and appraising. The cramped dimensions of the room surprised Olivia. A desk, littered with the standard collection of photo frames and computer accessories, encroached on the floor space, leaving Olivia and her inquisitors almost uncomfortably close. "It was so small," she recalls. "It was just someone's office."

The mundane setting contrasted with the importance of the event taking place there. This was the final-round interview for the prestigious Jefferson Scholarship—an award that covered the full costs of attending the University of Virginia. Three months earlier, Olivia had been nominated by her high school for the prize. She had survived a round of regional interviews before being flown down to Charlottesville, Virginia—home to the university—for a battery of tests leading up to this interview. Over the past two days, Olivia had taken exams to assess her math and writing skills. She had also been given a packet of academic papers to read, and then placed in a conference room to debate their merits with other finalists while members of the Jefferson Scholars Foundation selection committee took notes. This final interview, however, held the most weight for the senior members of the foundation who would decide whether or not Olivia was Jefferson material.

To better understand what constitutes Jefferson material, consider a student whom I'll call Laura Gant, who won the scholarship the previous year. Laura liked to write. As a high school student she interned at *Business Week* and had several pieces published on the magazine's Web site. She also won the Victor L. Ridder Scholarship, the National Council of Teachers of English Achievement Award in Writing, and the Harvard-Radcliff Book Award. Not surprising, she boasted exceptional grades that had earned her an almost embarrassingly long list of academic awards and scholarships. In addition, she's an artist and a talented musician—both voice and piano—who studied her craft seriously at a special music school in New York State. She rounded out her activity list by being the copresident of a school club, a member of the National Honor Society, and the cofounder of a community service group, and she was heavily involved in both the theater and choir groups at her high school.

Laura is a sterling example of the standard thinking about college admissions. She distinguished herself in high school by demonstrating commitment to lots of activities. Her life, I imagine, must have been brutal—a constant stream of work driven by the persistent fear of falling short of perfection. In the end, however, the suffering paid off when she won the Jefferson. This is the type of student against whom Olivia had to compete.

Olivia had never heard of Laura Gant, and this was probably for the best. Olivia's extracurricular involvements looked nothing like Laura's. Olivia didn't win armfuls of awards. She was not a star musician or an artist. She didn't start any organizations, or, for that matter, even participate in that many. Here's what she did do: to satisfy her school's athletic requirement, she joined the dance team, a commitment that required only four to five hours a week.

"That was much better than the ten-plus hours you'd spend if you joined a real sports team," she told me.

During her senior year she joined the tech crew for the school musical, but this counted as an elective class. She also cochaired her senior class's community service organization.

"In past years, the group marched in parades and held bake sales," she recalls. "My coleader and I decided to not do that kind of thing. It really takes a lot of energy to organize high schoolers for things like that!"

Instead, she and her coleader shunted their classmates toward an existing community service program that organized a service trip that would take place soon after graduation.

"Leading that group required, on average, about two hours a week," Olivia says. "It was not a huge commitment at all."

During her sophomore summer, she was also a part-time unpaid volunteer at the University of New Hampshire's marine biology laboratory. (The professor who ran the lab was her family's next-door neighbor.) You'll learn more about what sparked her interest in marine biology later in Part 1; for now it's enough to know that she returned to the lab her junior summer as a paid research assistant and planned on doing the same her final summer before college.

And that's about it.

If you're keeping score, the above entailed six to seven hours of activities per week during the school year—leaving Olivia's afternoons, evenings, and weekends wonderfully free. She had more than enough time to keep up with her courses without resorting to late nights or experiencing stress. And this still left abundant time to relax. Olivia enjoyed her underscheduled lifestyle, and she looks back on high school fondly.

She was not Laura Gant.

On the surface, it seemed as if Olivia's prospects for winning the Jefferson Scholarship were dim. She had avoided the stress that comes from an overpacked schedule, but as she sat before the five men and women who would decide whether to grant her one of their alma mater's most prestigious honors, she worried that she was about to pay the price for her happiness.

"At the time I felt really insecure about it. Maybe I should have played varsity soccer and lacrosse and, you know, become student council president," she recalls.

Some pleasantries were exchanged, and then the interview began in earnest. "Tell me," one of the men said, "about those horseshoe crabs."

With this question, the fear vanished from Olivia's mind. She knew how to talk about horseshoe crabs. The past two summers, she had spent every morning and every afternoon commuting to and from the UNH campus with her neighbor, the director of the lab where she worked, holding lively debates about the nuances of marine biology.

"One morning—to give you an example—the professor began going on about a paper on particular neurotransmitters in the brain of lobsters," Olivia told me. "It wasn't his area of research, but he was fascinated anyway. It helped me understand that being a scientist isn't just about focusing on one small area; it can also be about being interested in huge, broad topics." This interest had seeped into Olivia's personal life, affecting what she read and what she thought about.

The interview conversation soon turned to a book Olivia had recently read for fun: *Emergence*, by Steven Johnson—a look at how large-scale complex traits can arise from small-scale simple actions; for example, how thousands of ants following simple rules aggregate into an intelligently run colony. Olivia began to riff about the book. She discussed how studying the emergent traits of horseshoe crab populations, as Johnson had described researchers doing with ants, might yield new clues about the behavior of the crustaceans. She wanted to study both marine biology and environmental science at college so she could tackle interdisciplinary problems of this kind.

Olivia's idea about emergence was original, but to her it was not particularly special. She loved the field of marine biology and was used to coming up with and debating ideas about it. This was simply what you did at the lab where she worked. It was a natural by-product of being genuinely interested in the subject.

The five scholarship committee members, however, were entranced. They were used to students, like Laura Gant, who would enter that cramped office and give careful, official-sounding answers to their questions—never failing to miss an opportunity to highlight accomplishments from their lengthy résumés. They would say things like "My time spent volunteering at the local hospital taught me the importance of service." Or, "Being student council president is another example of my ability to lead."

Olivia, on the other hand, ignored this strategy. She exuded confidence and curiosity. Above all, there was real substance behind her words. Put another way, she was actually interesting, and this would take her further than she ever imagined.

The next night, after returning home to New Hampshire, Olivia got the call. This student from a small high school—a student with copious free time, who had never won major academic awards or competitions, or started any important club or organization, and who lived a happy, low-stress life—was informed that she had won the scholarship.

As it turns out, Olivia's story of interestingness trumping busyness is not unique. In the next section you'll hear about another laid-back student who transformed a love of life into admissions success.

The Forty-Minute Essay

Jessica, a student attending a private school in Upstate New York, decided as a sophomore to adopt an underscheduled lifestyle. This decision was prompted by a short-lived, ill-fated brush with entrepreneurship the year before. She had been paying for a deluxe Web hosting account, when she had an idea. She could rent an entire Celeron server from the hosting company for $59 a month. She could then resell a hosting account for around $90 to $100. The difference would be profit, which she could use to help pay her own server bills.

Jessica rented and resold her first server, and then soon thought: "Why not do this with more computers and make even more profit?" She discovered that a P4 rack server bought for $400 could be rented for $180, generating an even bigger profit after the initial cost was paid back. So she bought one—and then some more.

Things soon got out of hand. First there was the logistics of handling money and client accounts. Even today, years later, Jessica hesitates to talk about what she did wrong during that crazy year. She never incorporated the business and didn't handle the money well. With thousands of dollars sloshing in and out of personal bank accounts, more servers being bought, and bills mounting, the finances became complicated, and that bred stress.

The human problems made things even worse. On paper, renting a server for one price and rerenting for a higher price seems like automatic money. What this equation omits, however, is the late-night phone calls, from the companies paying those higher prices, when something went wrong.

Things often went wrong.

Jessica started bringing her cell phone to school to answer tech support calls in between classes. Her anxiety rose. The situation came to a head on New Year's Eve in her freshman year.

Jessica was away for the holiday break with her family when her phone rang. "It was literally one minute before the ball was about to drop," she recalls. The call was from her business partner.

"Hey, big problems," he started. Jessica's stomach churned. "All of our customers just got their data wiped out by a hacker."

On the TV, the ball began its descent.

"I'm on vacation, can this—? Shit, this sounds really bad," Jessica replied.

It was possible that eight hundred companies had just lost their data. She knew the feeling well; earlier in the year the same thing had happened to the three hundred customers they had at the time. As the New Year officially began, Jessica punched in the number of the technician on call at the data center. It would be a long night.

A few months later Jessica found her way out of this self-created prison. A client offered to take over the servers and their accounts. Jessica wouldn't make any money from the deal, but the client would take on the outstanding bills. The agreement was made at five o'clock on a Tuesday morning over an MSN Web chat.

"It was sort of scary; it left a big gap in my life," Jessica recalls. "But it was also a relief. There is no way to describe what it's like."

The stress of this experience drove Jessica to vow that she would never lose control of her schedule again. She became wary, for example, about taking on too many commitments. She joined her school's model UN club and played in the jazz band. She also did some volunteering and was involved with student government. But these were her only formal activities. In fact, she even left most of these minor clubs off her college applications, explaining, "I thought they would clutter things." At the beginning of her junior year, she also started a blog to help work through some of her thoughts about the experience with entrepreneurship that had shaken up her freshman-year life. It was a way to stay connected to that world without actually running a company.

Jessica kept her academic demands equally light. "On a weekday, I might work until eight and then I was done," she told me. "I rarely worked on weekends. I would just hang out, work on my blog, or build random Web site stuff."

She was good at starting assignments early and taking advantage of slow periods to get ahead on her work. She was so good, in fact, that by her junior year she would often finish her homework for the week *as early as Tuesday evening*, leaving the rest of the week completely free for her to do whatever she wanted.

"It was such a relaxed time," she recalls.

Jessica was about as far from a grind as it is possible to be without failing out of school. So when it came to writing her college application essay for Berkeley, one of her dream schools, it didn't cross her mind to obsess over the task. Fortunately, Jessica had some experience with writing. Her blog had led her to devote much of her free time to informally reading and thinking about entrepreneurship and talking to interesting people involved with it. As I'll explain, it was this thinking and writing that made her genuinely interesting, and it was her interestingness that would make her application so unique and powerful—helping her get into this notoriously competitive school.

To understand this point, let's start with the breed of standard application essay that Jessica was competing with. In 2005, for example, a student included an essay titled "Leadership Experiences" with her application to Berkeley. The essay opened:

After being selected as a delegate to the Freedom Foundation Leadership Conference at Valley Forge, I agonized over whether it would be worth missing a week of school and work. However, the trip exceeded my highest expectations. My opinions, notoriously hard to change, were refreshingly challenged as I debated and discussed controversial issues.

In 2006, another student submitted an essay titled "The Antidote to the Troubles of Life," which began:

> I was out of my element. Alcoholic fathers and abusive mothers? Gangs and drugs?! I had been thrust, suddenly, into the real world, exposed to all its horrors. It was two years ago that I had first entered the confirmation program at my church. The two-year program was designed to prepare me . . .

Most of the roughly thirty-six thousand essays that pass before the bleary eyes of the Berkeley admissions staff each year follow the well-worn format of these two examples: choose your most impressive activity; tell a story about how the activity helped you develop a trait you think the admissions officers care about; if possible, work in passing references to other items from your brag sheet. Bonus points are awarded, of course, if you can start the essay with a dash of first-person, new-journalism-style description ("I was out of my element . . ."). After reading a collection of these essays while researching this book, I developed some serious sympathy for the Berkeley admissions staff. This stuff is brutally bland and predictable.

It's safe to assume that most of these thirty-six thousand applicants obsessed over their essays—perhaps, in many cases, hiring professional counselors to tweak the words. This obsession makes sense for one simple reason: Berkeley is incredibly difficult to get into. In its 2009 rankings, *U.S. News & World Report* named it the top public school in the nation and put it at number twenty-one among all universities in the United States.

Berkeley has an acceptance rate that hovers around 20 percent, and if the applicant doesn't live in California, that percentage drops. The average GPA of Berkeley's freshman class is 3.94, and, not surprisingly, basically every admitted student (98 percent) is near the top of his or her high school class.

These numbers tell a chilling story: grades alone won't cut it. Your essay, perhaps your only chance the harried admissions staff will get to learn something about your personality and your accomplishments, is crucial. This is why the authors of essays like "Leadership Experiences" and "The Antidote to the Troubles of Life" invest so much time in making sure that their essay says all of the right things.

Jessica never got the memo about the standard format for college essays and the time supposedly required to write such things properly. She's embarrassed to admit that she spent only forty minutes on her Berkeley essay. And yet it still sparkled in a way that "Leadership Experiences" and "The Antidote to the Troubles of Life" did not. To understand why, let's turn our attention to the progression of Jessica's blog.

Her initial blog articles reflected on her experience running her company and her plans for the future. For example, an early post, from March 2007, discussed her struggle with the fact that her mom called her business ideas "boring."

"I mean, what do you say to that?" she asked in the post's conclusion.

In April, she talked about the difficulties of a teenager wanting to run a company. Once again her mom plays a central role. "My mom lectured me for a few hours. She told me that I needed a foundation to my life," Jessica reported. She then went on to debate the merits of going to college versus trying to start another business.

This honesty attracted a small but loyal following, which helped connect Jessica to dozens of interesting personalities from the world of entrepreneurship. She told me a story, for example, about a memorable afternoon spent with the president of a San Francisco–based tech company where she had been a summer intern (a job that she would not have had without her blog).

"We were sitting out on a beach. We weren't talking about business, it was a friendly chat, talking about philosophy, and what happens when you die, the meaning of life, how to build meaningful relationships."

These mentors and experiences helped Jessica's thinking mature. This, in turn, helped her writing. "My first few blog posts were stupid and amateurish; I was pretty arrogant back then," she recalls. "But soon, I was like, 'Shit, I haven't run a company since the end of ninth grade; I'm bragging about something I did years ago.' That's when I started to change my blog posts. . . . I talked a lot about my failures instead of my successes." As her writing talent grew, so did her audience. By the time she applied to Berkeley, her blog was drawing more than thirty-five thousand unique visitors each month. Her maturity was what gave Jessica's essay, dashed off in forty minutes, a presence and confidence that couldn't be matched by most of the cookie-cutter dreck that passes before the admissions officers' tired eyes.

"I wrote my essay about the experiences I had, and what I learned from them, how they influenced my life," she said. "It wasn't all pristine stories." In other words, it was truthful and not self-promoting; it was the type of writing she had polished on her blog. Instead of filling her essay with melodrama—"I was standing in the homeless shelter, realizing for the first time how cushy my life had been"—she was direct about the size of her business and the difficulties it created, discussing, among other things, the frequency with which clients broke their contracts and the constant battle against those trying to take advantage of her venture. "As part of the company's day-to-day operations," she wrote, "we often had to look into issues of copyright infringement and cyberfraud." She ended by reflecting on the lessons learned from watching her customers' efforts to exploit loopholes in their contracts, concluding: "While there is a difference between morality and law, the two often coincide."

Her essay was genuinely interesting. Because of this, she was one of the lucky 20 percent accepted into Berkeley that spring. She earned a place even though she was applying from out of state and had a spotty transcript (during her freshman-year business debacle, for example, she earned only a C average), a lax activity load (at least by Berkeley standards), and a high school life she actually enjoyed. Genuine interest had once again trumped the factors that most students obsess over.

2

Rethinking "Passion"

WHY ARE Olivia and Jessica so impressive? It's a simple question, but seeking the answer yields important insights about the relaxed superstar lifestyle.

Here's what we know: they ignored the standard admissions strategy of showing commitment to as many activities as possible. Indeed, both Olivia and Jessica enjoyed an exceptional amount of free time, so something else must have driven their impressiveness. What was it? Most students, if asked, would have a ready answer to our question. "It's obvious," they'd say. "Those students did well because they showed real *passion*."

Ah, "passion"—perhaps the most dreaded and obnoxious word in all of college admissions. What student or parent doesn't experience shivers of annoyance upon hearing a college counselor advise, "You need to find your passion," or an admissions officer chirp, "We're looking for passionate students"?

Twenty years ago, this term wasn't even in the admissions vocabulary. Back then, the rules were much simpler. Colleges made it clear that they were looking for "well-rounded" students. If you had top grades, played a varsity sport, and were president of the student body, you could go to an Ivy League school. But then the population boom dubbed Gen Y started to graduate from high school, and a knowledge-worker economy began to place more importance on the name gracing your diploma. Schools were soon deluged with "well-rounded" students and began having to turn away the type of applicant who used to be an automatic accept. At this point, the process plunged into mystery. The emphasis on "well-rounded" faded, and in its place rose the shadowy concept of the "passionate" applicant. This hopelessly ambiguous concept has since evolved into a catchall explanation for any student who gets into college for doing something that does not obviously require a great amount of hard work or natural ability.

You don't need the idea of "passion," for example, to explain why the young woman who played violin at Carnegie Hall got into Princeton, or the Olympic swimmer got into Stanford; they both did really hard things that required lots of natural talent. But when you turn to students like Olivia and Jessica, things become murky. There's no obvious supertalent or large amount of hard work in their stories, so what makes them stand out? This is where most people instinctively deploy the "p"-word—it provides some rationale to an otherwise inscrutable process.

But when you think a little harder, the nagging question remains: *What the hell does "passion" mean?*

I've heard numerous answers. An education columnist I know proposed that "passion" means you invest a lot of effort over a long period of time in a single activity. When I asked this question of a group of students at Wellesley High School, a competitive public school tucked away in the Boston suburbs, I received a variety of responses ranging from "something different

than what other people are doing" to "something outside of the
structure of the school." The admissions advice site Accepted
.com went further, reducing the concept to a concrete formula:
"Passion = Action + Dedication."

Olivia and Jessica satisfy most of these varying definitions.
They invested effort over a long period of time, and their pursuits
were unusual and outside the structure of the school. But I've
met many other students who met the same criteria yet still did
not do well in the admissions process. Consider the following
two examples:

* **Peter:** Spent his summers volunteering with a veterinarian.
* **Nathan:** Took glockenspiel lessons for many years.

Peter and Nathan also satisfy our proposed definitions for "passion." Each persistently worked on an unusual activity, outside
the structure of the school, over a long period of time. Yet they
don't generate the same sense of impressiveness as Olivia and
Jessica. Their passions seem constructed, as if they'd read the
definitions offered above and then systematically identified pursuits that would meet the criteria. It's passion reduced to a recipe:
"Add one part unusual, mix in half a cup of persistence . . ." To
put it more bluntly, you read their activity descriptions, and then
you yawn.

This brings us back to our original question, which I can
now reword as: What was it, exactly, about Olivia and Jessica
that made them pop out as compared to students like Peter and
Nathan? Here's my suggestion: let's abandon the word "passion"
once and for all. It's been overused and underdefined for too
long. If we are going to crack the relaxed superstar code, we need
to start from scratch with something more precise.

With this in mind, I'll begin with the following claim, generated from studying many students like Olivia and Jessica:

> **The Interestingness Hypothesis, Part 1**
> When admissions officers say they're looking for students who show "passion," what they really mean is that they're looking for the type of student who would appeal to an NPR talk show producer. That is, a student who could sit down and chat about a topic for thirty minutes and hold an educated audience's rapt attention.

I call this trait *interestingness*. Peter and Nathan didn't have it. It's possible that Peter has some fascinating insights to share about the care of animals, but, more likely, this activity was just the standard reluctant high school volunteering gig taken on because the student thinks it looks good on his résumé. An interview with Peter would be dull. The same holds for Nathan: "I like the glockenspiel because, uh, well, it's different, and, well, uh— Do you know when the Harvard admissions deadline is?"

Olivia and Jessica, on the other hand, make fascinating interview subjects. In fact, this is exactly what got Olivia the Jefferson Scholarship: she held the attention of the interviewing committee with her musing on the future of population biology. *It was truly interesting stuff!* The same holds for Jessica. She spent so much time immersed in the ideas swirling around the new dotcom revolution that she developed thoughts that were actually worth listening to—a fact confirmed by the thirty thousand to forty thousand readers who visit her blog each month.

In other words, Olivia and Jessica did well in the admissions process not because their activities took lots of time, or were unusual, or were outside the structure of the school, but because they transformed Olivia and Jessica into students who possessed the important trait of interestingness. The trait permeated their essays, recommendations, and scholarship interviews, and this made them stand out.

Let's pause for a moment to take stock. I just tossed out the concept of "passion" and replaced it with the more precise concept of "interestingness." This solution, however, only gets us halfway there. You might agree that interestingness is important, and that it helped Olivia and Jessica, but this leads to an equally important follow-up question: *Why* did their activities generate this trait? Or, *How* does one get interestingness?

Allow me to introduce my second claim:

> **The Interestingness Hypothesis, Part 2**
> Interestingness cannot be forced or planned in advance. It is generated, instead, as a natural by-product of a "deep interest," which is a long-term pursuit that a student returns to *voluntarily* and *eagerly* whenever given a chance.

An easy method to determine whether a pursuit is a deep interest is to apply the *Saturday-morning test*. Imagine you wake up refreshed on a Saturday morning and realize you have no obligations for the day. Is your first instinct to spend time on the pursuit in question? If so, it's probably a deep interest. If instead you're happy to have some time to finally relax, then the pursuit is probably something you're doing just because you think it looks good. Peter and Nathan, we imagine, wouldn't rearrange their schedules or give up sleep on Saturday morning to volunteer extra hours at the vet or break out the glockenspiel for a good long practice session. Those activities were carefully chosen résumé boosters, not true deep interests.

Olivia and Jessica, on the other hand, saw their pursuits as something they wanted to do—the pursuits were inseparable from their definition of relaxation. Reading biology books was Olivia's idea of fun. Whenever financially feasible, Jessica dedicated her school vacations to flying out to Silicon Valley to meet tech entrepreneurs and attend conferences (she gained online notoriety for her ability to gain last-minute access to tech conferences without tickets). During the rest of the year, she had to content herself with having phone conversations and reading articles. In both cases, the pursuits were what these two young women most wanted to do with their free time.

This is an important point, worth reiterating: it's not the activity that matters, but rather the effect the activity has on your personality. This is why the standard definitions of passion fail to consistently explain why some students are accepted and some are not. The old definitions focused on the characteristics of the activities, not the traits of the students. If you arbitrarily pick an activity and stick with it to demonstrate your persistence, you're probably wasting your time. Such assembly-line passions are unlikely to generate interestingness, so you'll remain yet another applicant who is showing little more than a strong desire to get accepted into college. For an admissions officer trying to build an interesting class, the fact that you're persistent or diligent means little. You might as well use those extra hours to improve your SAT score, which would have a bigger impact in the end. On the other hand, if you have a true deep interest, you'll develop the personality trait of interestingness. This will infuse your application. To this same admissions officer, you'll pop out as exactly the type of person who can make a class exciting. The best part, of course, is that this magic trait has nothing to do with hard work or natural talent—recall the easy schedules of Olivia and Jessica—which is why it's so central to the relaxed superstar lifestyle.

So *forget passion!* I've replaced this outdated concept with a much more specific set of marching orders: *Develop a deep interest.*

But we're not out of the woods yet. Next, I'll disprove the myth that deep interests are not available to all.

The Myth of the Naturally Interest-Prone Student

When most students first encounter a real deep interest—for example, they hear about Olivia's marine biology obsession—they progress through three predictable stages. First, they scan their own life and ask, "What am I interested in that could be transformed into a deep interest?" Second, they fail to find anything. Third, they conclude that students like Olivia and Jessica are somehow just special. Perhaps they were just born more *naturally interest-prone* than the rest of us poor average mortals. After passing through these three stages, most students then sigh in resignation, acknowledge that their only hope is to outwork all the other applicants, and then go join the key club. With this in mind, if I'm going to convince you that interestingness should be a big part of your college admissions strategy, I must first debunk the hypothesis that only special students can develop a deep interest.

Supporters of this hypothesis would not be surprised to hear about an intriguing data set gathered from four school districts in rural Pennsylvania. In 2001, a research team, led by Professor Linda Caldwell of Penn State University, subjected junior high school students from these districts to an alphabet soup of acronymized psychological tests—tests bearing exciting names such as the FTMS-A (Free Time Motivation Scale for Adolescents) and the always-popular LEB-A (Leisure Experience Battery for Adolescents). Each was designed to tease out information about how the students spent their time and for what reasons. On one of the tests, for example, the students faced statement after statement such as "For me, free time just drags on and on," "My free-time activities are very interesting to me," and "[I'm involved with this activity] because I want people to like me." They were asked to assign a value to each statement from a five-point scale that ranged from "strongly disagree" to "strongly agree."

Once the scores were gathered, aggregated, and pushed through sophisticated statistical models, a remarkable finding emerged. Within this group of junior high school students was a smaller subgroup, the *subject group*, that showed significant differences from their classmates. As Caldwell later described it in a 2004 paper reporting the results of the study, the subject group showed "higher levels of interest (and thus lower levels of boredom) than the comparison group." Members of the subject group also "scored higher than the comparison group on initiative . . . the ability to restructure boring situations . . . and the ability to plan and make decisions in free time." These students "reported participating in new and interesting activities more often than the students in the comparison group" and overall showed "higher levels of well-being" (psychologist-speak for "they were happier").

Put another way, this subject group seems to support the claim that some students are more naturally interest-prone than others—they gravitated toward things that they really liked; they were more likely to take initiative and start new projects; and they were skilled at transforming free time into something productive or exciting. These students remind us of Olivia and Jessica—they are excited by the world and seem destined to develop deep interests. This sounds like bad news for the average student who isn't naturally stumbling into fascinating projects and causes. Perhaps deep interests are just not in the cards for most of us.

Not so fast!

I have a confession. In my above description of the study, I left out a key piece of information. It's true that Caldwell and her team identified a subject group that scored much higher than the comparison group on traits related to interest development. The tests, which were conducted in the spring of 2001, produced results that were clear and conclusive. What I didn't mention, however, was that these same students were also tested six months earlier, in the fall of 2000. Here's where things get interesting. During the first testing session, there were *no differences* between the subject group and the rest of the students. That is, in the fall of 2000 all of the students exhibited roughly the same low levels of interest and high levels of boredom. This leads to a powerful conclusion: the subject-group students weren't born more naturally interest-prone than the other students. They were transformed. Most remarkably, this transformation required only a few short months. The ability to attract deep interests, therefore, is not necessarily an inborn trait; it can also be learned.

For the students in the subject group, at the core of their transformation was a six-lesson curriculum dubbed TimeWise. The goal of the program was to teach students how to make better use of their leisure time. Its immediate goal was to reduce drug use—bored and uninterested students are more likely to fall into dangerous behaviors. Its larger motivation, however, was the conviction of a growing number of researchers, including Linda Caldwell, that having abundant leisure time, and using this leisure time properly, provides a powerful tool for building a happy, impressive, and healthy life.

The ideas taught in the TimeWise lessons were simple. For example, one lesson gave advice about balancing what one "has to do" with what one "wants to do." Another lesson provided strategies for following up on something that seems interesting. At the start of the program, the students created a diary to track how they spent their time. Later they went back to analyze the diaries and identify places where they should have done things differently. And so on.

Amazingly, these simple lessons made a big difference. Adding basic direction and structure to their free time was enough to turn these bored teenagers into genuinely interesting people.

When it comes to living a fascinating life, we're not constrained by our genes. It's instead something that with the right instruction anyone can choose to do.

The Interest-Prone Life

Intrigued by this research, I called Professor Caldwell to find out more about what the average student can do to build an interest-prone life. Though simple, the lessons used in the TimeWise program were too numerous for easy summary. I asked her if she could reduce the approach into something more pithy.

"We know you need to find things that you're truly interested in," she told me. "The problem is that students don't know in advance what these are."

This initial failure to immediately identify a potential deep interest often causes students to abandon their efforts. Caldwell, however, is perhaps the world expert on how students can overcome this initial hurdle and continue to develop toward an interest-prone life. I was eager to learn her secrets.

"You need to be exposed to many things—you should expose yourself even though you might not know if you'll be interested: find out about and attend events on the local college campus and in your community, and ask yourself, 'Did I enjoy this?'"

She added that this exposure should be tempered by what researchers call "casual leisure time": free time dedicated to undistracted reflection and relaxation. Or, as Caldwell describes it, "time when you turn off the phone and the instant messenger and take a walk to appreciate the world without something in your ear."

Unfortunately, in this age of admissions hysteria, many students' instinct is to do the exact opposite of this. Instead of keeping lots of free time open to expose themselves to different things, and sometimes just relax and reflect, they try to fill every

free minute with schoolwork and activities, all in an attempt to
outdo their admissions competition.

Caldwell is not amused.

"I think eliminating leisure time from your schedule is the
worst possible thing a student could do," she said. In fact, a 2007
study of students in a suburban high school found that "the
greater the amount of time students reported participating in
[structured] activities . . . the higher their self-reported level of
anxiety."

The researchers found that activities by themselves are not bad;
it's the "overscheduling" of these activities that causes problems.
They conclude: "These increasing obligations and time demands
are cutting into adolescents' leisure experiences, which are critical
for helping them discover their identities and release stress."

In other words, if you want to be stressed and anxious, then
follow the standard strategy of packing as much as possible into
your schedule. But if you want to attract deep interests, and
therefore maximize your chance of generating both interestingness and a happy life, then, according to Professor Caldwell, you
should do the following:

1. Leave plenty of leisure time in your schedule.
2. Use this time to expose yourself to *lots* of different things,
   even if you're not sure in advance whether they'll interest
   you.
3. Leave some of this time free to relax and reflect "without
   something in your ear."

The superstars I interviewed stumbled into this behavior, and
were reaping the rewards when they began the college process.
But as Caldwell's research shows, it doesn't matter whether you
naturally gravitate toward an underscheduled lifestyle or artificially impose it—either way, you'll attract deep interests.

In the next chapter, I return to the stories of Olivia and Jessica. This time, however, I turn back the clock to reveal the sequence of events that led to the development of their deep interests. The goal is to show you what the underscheduled lifestyle looks like in practice.

3

The Making of a Relaxed Superstar

YOU'VE ALREADY seen how the power of interestingness—generated by deep interests—propelled two underscheduled students into their reach schools. As I noted in Chapter 2, Professor Linda Caldwell explained that deep interests are attracted if you maintain free time and use it to explore. Here, I put these theories to the test by rewinding the stories of Olivia and Jessica back to their start to show you how these two students became superstars.

How Olivia Became a Superstar

Olivia's story begins during the spring of her sophomore year of high school. She was assigned a project on New Hampshire's Great Bay tidal estuary, a vast pool of seawater, over 150 miles in diameter, that sits 10 miles inland from the New Hampshire Atlantic coast. Most people have never heard of the Great Bay, but to a marine biologist, the ecosystems of its waters and the surrounding marshes are a source of endless fascination.

For her project—a poster for her chemistry class—Olivia was tasked with showing the role of nitrogen in the Great Bay life cycle. The details of her poster elude her today, but what she does remember is that her teacher singled out her work for praise, giving her an A+.

During the course of her work on the chemistry project, her parents had mentioned that their next-door neighbor was a marine biologist at the nearby University of New Hampshire. Olivia didn't know much about his research, but she was aware that "he did something cool with lobsters." Inspired by the praise she received for her project, she decided, on a whim, to send him an e-mail.

"I asked if he needed an unpaid summer volunteer," Olivia recalls. She was fueled by romantic visions of wading through a tidal estuary, the sun dipping low to the horizon, a research notebook in her hand. But her hopes were also balanced with pragmatism. "I assumed there was probably some sort of policy against bringing in random volunteers."

There wasn't. The professor replied that he would be happy to take on some free help.

A couple of months later, as summer began, Olivia joined her neighbor for the short drive to the Durham campus of the University of New Hampshire. She had arranged to work thirty hours a week as a volunteer, with another twenty hours dedicated to her standard summer waitress job—her only chance to make money for the year. When they arrived at Redmond Hall, home to the biology and zoology departments, she followed the professor up the stairs to his second-floor laboratory.

"Right away he introduced me to this graduate student I would be working with," Olivia recalls. The student, a T-shirted young man in his twenties, led her to a small room. Low tables lining the walls were stacked haphazardly with videotapes. In the center was a TV, a stool, and, strangely enough, a clear plastic ruler. He pointed Olivia toward a seat before saying, "Okay, here's what you're going to do."

He put the first tape in a player wired to the TV. It took Olivia a second to orient herself to the scene. It was the ocean floor—seaweed waving, patterns of diffuse light dancing across the sand. In the middle of the shot was the end of a large-diameter white PVC pipe. A multidigit time code raced furiously in the corner.

Plop.

A lobster fell through the pipe's opening and onto the sand.

"Watch the seaweed," the graduate student said. "When it moves, we need to know how much, and when it happened. See, like there!"

He paused the tape. Ignoring the lobster, which had begun to move out of the frame, he demonstrated how to rewind the recording, frame by frame, and then measure the movement of the seaweed by holding the plastic ruler up to the screen. He showed her how to record the movement in a logbook.

Olivia sneaked a glance at the piles of tapes that littered the room, then turned back to accept the ruler from the graduate student.

It was going to be a long summer.

Sometime during that first week, she ran into an unexpected character in the group's common room. He was a New Hampshire lobsterman. In contrast to the slender, pale students who populated the lab, this visitor stood out. His skin was tanned and weather-beaten, his back knotted with the muscles forged from pulling waterlogged traps from the ocean floor. The professor greeted the man warmly, and the two quickly fell into conversation. Olivia heard them discussing lobster yields. As she later learned, the lobsterman worked with the professor, assisting in research projects aimed at keeping the local lobster fishery viable. People in the lobster-fishing community were often suspicious of scientists, whom they associated with the heavy-handed and often economically disastrous regulations passed down by the New England Fisheries Management Council. But over the years, due to the hundreds of hours that the professor, and more than a few seasick young graduate students, had spent on their boats counting stock and talking shop, trust had formed.

At this point, Olivia's thinking changed. Her volunteer work was not glamorous, but seeing the lobsterman helped her connect the studies to important issues that affected real people's lives. The field of marine biology was transforming from a passing interest into something more important. It was no longer the momentary whim of a sixteen-year-old girl excited by a grade on a chemistry poster. It was turning into a true deep interest.

She recommitted to her work, boring as it was, and began to gain the respect of the team. The next winter, she received an unexpected call from the professor. He had discovered that his latest National Science Foundation grant included money for a special program aimed at hiring female and minority high school students to work in the laboratories.

"He asked if I would be interested in coming back to the lab the next summer and actually earning a salary," Olivia recalls. She quickly agreed.

That second summer, Olivia graduated from measuring the movement of seaweed to working on the migration patterns of horseshoe crabs. Over the past few years, the lab had used radio beacons to track the movement of a large number of these crabs across the rocky bottom of the Great Bay. Olivia's job was to connect the movement of the crabs with movement of the tides, as shown in a tide table. If there was a pattern—say, every time the tide went out, the crabs retreated—this would substantiate the professor's hunch that the crabs used the tides to coordinate. If not, it would hint that something else was going on. The work may not have matched her original vision of wading into the brackish bay marshes, observing animals in their natural state, but it was real science as real science is done today: sifting through data and hunting for patterns. Her intellectual confidence grew.

Olivia's second summer culminated with a presentation at the lab's weekly research meeting. She remembers counting the hours before the talk with nervous apprehension. When she finally stood up in front of her PowerPoint slides, however, and began to walk the assembled students and postdoctoral fellows through her findings on tide levels and crab movements, she soon found her voice.

"I know this stuff," she realized.

The audience treated her like a peer.

By the time Olivia applied to college, and was nominated for the Jefferson Scholarship, her deep interest in marine biology had taken root. When she sat down for her interview, her confidence and enthusiasm for the subject helped her radiate the interestingness that won her the prize, even though her schedule was far less demanding than that of the standard applicant.

Deconstructing Olivia's Story

Olivia's story provides strong support for Linda Caldwell's theory of how deep interests develop. As a sophomore, Olivia had an open schedule and an instinct to explore things that caught her attention. When her chemistry teacher praised her project on the Great Bay, Olivia thought, "Maybe I'd like this stuff. I'll give it a try." If she had been an overscheduled student, her summer would already have been filled with expensive international mission trips and sessions at college summer-enrichment programs. But she wasn't that kind of student, and was instead able to easily work the volunteer spot into her schedule when it was offered. From here, the momentary interest eventually transformed into a deep interest, and all the hoped-for benefits followed.

What's important to notice is what *didn't* happen in Olivia's story. At no point did she sit down and say, "I am passionate about marine biology; I will now dedicate my high school life to this cause so I can get into the University of Virginia." She had no idea that this field of study would blossom into such an important part of her life. In fact, if she had originally set up the volunteering gig with the clear intent of improving her admissions chances, it's safe to assume that she wouldn't have gotten nearly as far. The rapid growth in her lab responsibilities and the abundance of outside reading and thinking she did on related topics—two key factors in the development of the interesting-ness that got her into UVA—resulted from the authentic interest she radiated toward the lab's work.

What Olivia did do was maintain free time and use it to explore things that seemed interesting. Eventually, as Professor Caldwell would have predicted, something stuck. As we move on to the origin story of Jessica, we find that, as with Olivia, the initial steps toward her deep interest also required a mixture of free time and luck.

How Jessica Became a Superstar

During spring break of her junior year of high school, Jessica visited the tropical island of Jamaica on vacation with her step-dad. On a sun-drenched Caribbean morning, Jessica's stepdad returned from a round of golf with an excited smile on his face. "I met this guy, Morris, on the course," he said. "He's involved in the tech industry. I think you two should meet." Jessica was intrigued. She hadn't given much thought to high-tech entre-preneurship since her stressful freshman-year experience, but the meeting sounded fun. "Why not?" she thought.

The next day, Jessica and Morris found each other on the beach. It turns out that the young man, still in his late twenties, had just sold his Internet start-up, Rackspace.com, for a sizable amount of money. He was vacationing in Jamaica to celebrate. This whiff of high-tech success captivated Jessica. Rackspace.com, she discovered, was a larger, more successful version of the same basic business idea she had pursued as a freshman. Meeting Morris was like a glimpse of an alternative reality—what might have happened if she had known what she was doing when she started her server business. Since giving up her company, Jessica had been licking her wounds. She was living an intentionally underscheduled life, wary of letting anything else dominate her schedule as the business had. But that afternoon on the beach, it was as if a misaligned gear had clicked back into place: Jessica's interest in entrepreneurship was back.

"I did everything I could to pick his brain," she recalls. "I asked him about getting started, about getting funding, about hiring people, about the growing pains, about going to college, about making use of college, about dropping out of college, about everything I could think of." The next day Jessica had lunch with Morris and his brother-in-law (also an entrepreneur, he had cofounded a semiconductor company), and the interrogation continued. Somewhere along the way they began prodding her to get out to the Bay Area, where it was all happening, and experience the heart of the tech industry in person.

Less than two months after returning from Jamaica, Jessica was on a plane to California for her first visit to Silicon Valley. Her itinerary was full. In the preceding six weeks, inspired by her beach encounter, she had been reaching out to every hot tech company in the valley, trying to arrange a meeting or even just get permission to hang around the company offices and experience life in a high-stakes start-up. She sent an e-mail to the founders of Reddit, a popular social news Web site, and ended up spending an afternoon in the Reddit offices. Out of the blue, she contacted Marc Benioff, the famously loudmouthed founder of the influential Salesforce.com. He passed her on to a well-connected young CEO he knew, who, in turn, met with Jessica and set her up with many more meetings. At the time, an entertainment start-up, Justin.TV, was beginning to make waves. Jessica convinced them to let her hang out and watch Justin, the star of one of the company's top shows, film a live feed.

"The people I've met through these trips have become incredible mentors," Jessica said. One of these connections, for example, was the president of the Web start-up PBwiki (now PBworks), with whom Jessica arranged an internship for the upcoming summer.

By the time Jessica returned from this first trip, she had trans-formed herself into a budding Silicon Valley insider. Bolstered by the confidence she'd developed, she started her entrepreneurship blog. The ability to report on conversations with top business personalities, and to bounce her ideas off of these experts, gave her credibility that attracted readers and increased her influence.

"It's like an endless cycle of goodness," Jessica explained. "You meet this person from your blog and they introduce you to other friends, or get you into events, and that leads you to something else."

By the time Jessica applied to Berkeley, this "cycle of good-ness" had made her into a minor celebrity within the world of high-tech entrepreneurship. In March 2008, for example, the Web site Valleywag, perhaps the most influential (and most vicious) repository of tech industry gossip, posted an article about how Jessica, then seventeen years old, had managed to gain an invitation to the ultraexclusive TED Conference, while some of the biggest names in the valley were not invited. (The article, satirically titled "After 17-year-old gets into TED, Michael Arrington now on Suicide Watch," poked fun at Arrington, the founder of the popular TechCrunch Web site.) And this is only one of the *eight* different articles appearing on Valleywag to date that mention Jessica—a strong indicator of her surprising visibility in Silicon Valley.

Of course, being an important player in the high-tech industry gave Jessica an aura of interestingness that few of the other thirty-six thousand applicants to Berkeley that year could match. After reviewing yet another application of a student in the top 5 percent of his class, who joined half-a-dozen clubs and took an absurd number of AP courses, the admissions officers must have sighed in hearty gratitude when they flipped to the story of a student who had snuck into important conferences, enjoyed late-night chats with powerful CEOs, and knew how to write about these experiences in a compelling manner.

"Finally," they may have thought. "Someone *interesting*."

Her mediocre grades and open, relaxed schedule were washed away in this tide of interestingness.

Deconstructing Jessica's Story

What strikes me most about Jessica's path is how much pivots on that chance encounter on a Jamaican golf course. I asked Jessica about this. "Having luck is important," she said. "But making extensive use of your luck is even more important."

This sentiment matches the theories of Linda Caldwell. Use free time to explore, but then *follow up* on the most interesting experiences. This acts like a systematic search for luck. You don't know in advance which chance encounter can spark a transformation in your life, but by seeking out lots of chance encounters you're increasing the probability that you'll stumble into the right one.

Jessica's difficult experience with her freshman-year company instilled a desire to keep her schedule open and flexible. When she met that young entrepreneur on the beach in Jamaica, and found her interest piqued by his tales of high-tech success, her open schedule allowed her to follow up aggressively—transforming a moment of inspiration into a true deep interest. If she had been the typical overscheduled student with an eye toward getting into Berkeley, this transformation would have been unlikely.

4

The Systematic Superstar

PERCHED HIGH up in the Santa Monica Mountains, near the final ascent of North Sepulveda Boulevard, is the Skirball Cultural Center. Its architecture is a mix of the modern and the ancient Semitic. Clad in horizontal strips of concrete and pink stone, it contrasts pleasingly with the rolling mountain backdrop. It was no surprise that Claremont McKenna College chose this stunning venue, in March 2008, to launch its equally stunning $600 million capital campaign—the largest such campaign ever conceived by a liberal arts institution.

On the evening of March 16, the main theater, filled to capacity, darkened. The stage was dominated by a pair of oversized video projection screens, each twenty feet tall. The screens lit up, alternating between clips of students on one side and faculty on the other. A young man by the name of Ben Casnocha appeared on the student screen. He had a prominent, dimpled chin and the broad shoulders of a six-foot-five, 230-pound basketball player. These bold features were offset by a delicate pair of glasses that echoed the precision with which he chose his words:

"I founded my first company when I was in high school and wrote my first nonfiction book before starting college. My college counselor told me Claremont McKenna would be a perfect fit. Here, I'm learning how an intellectual foundation of history and philosophy can support my real-world experiences."

Ben's image froze on the screen while a clip featuring a professor began to play on its twin. The professor launched into a spiel about how the college supported and nurtured young talents like the impressive young man captured in a moment of still-frame contemplation on the screen beside him.

Ben's a superstar. There's no question about that. By the time he appeared on that screen he had written a book, made regular appearances on NPR, and given speeches across the country. When Ben's clip played that March evening, he was one of just a handful of students chosen to represent the best of Claremont McKenna at the gala. Even more amazing, Ben was only a freshman and had completed just a single semester of college. The day he arrived on campus, he had already been identified by the institution as one of its best.

There are two things about Ben that should interest you. First, fifteen months earlier, when he graduated from high school and set off on a precollege gap year, he was not a superstar—he had not written a book or become a radio personality or a popular speaker. If he had gone straight from high school to Claremont, the college probably would not have selected him to help kick off its record-breaking capital campaign. Second, during the year that launched him into stardom, Ben lived according to a simple experiment designed to answer this question: What would happen if you built your entire life around the law of underscheduling? The answer turned out to be *a lot*.

This story is important, as it previews your own trajectory if you decide to apply the systematic advice in the upcoming play-book. Whereas Olivia and Jessica naturally gravitated toward the underscheduled lifestyle, the strategies that follow teach you how to artificially inject this philosophy into your daily routine. Ben's story will prove that this proactive approach can provide fantastic results much faster than you may believe possible.

The Experiment

When Ben graduated from high school, in the spring of 2006, he had inconsistent grades and a busy extracurricular schedule dominated by an unusual pursuit: he had founded a technology business, Comcate, Inc. The concept started as a class project for a junior high school technology elective. Ben and his fellow students were challenged by their teacher to come up with a useful Web site. They soon settled on a problem of great importance to teenage baseball fans from the San Francisco area: the rundown condition of the stadium seats at Candlestick Park. Ben recalls thinking, "These seats are just plain dirty; there should be a way for citizens to efficiently complain about such civic travesties." Because he knew something about building Web sites, he kept working on the idea after the class concluded. "I learned that local government is no good at handling complaints," Ben recalls. "So I thought, Why not start a company to help them deal with these issues?" Comcate, Inc. was born.

The company grew into a solid small business. It acquired clients and employees, and it still exists today, though Ben has given up his role in its day-to-day operations. The business, combined with traditional activities like editing the school newspaper and playing on the varsity basketball team, no doubt helped Ben get into Claremont, but it was not enough to transform him into a superstar. Due in large part to the demands of his business, Ben earned only a 2.67 GPA and SAT scores that were "good, not great." His college counselor once told him: "I'm going to be blunt, your numbers will hurt the averages of [the top] schools. . . . You're facing an uphill battle."

Ben was burned-out and disappointed by an admissions process that placed many of the nation's top schools out of reach for him, even though he was an obviously talented student. Around this time he wrote on his blog, "Let's face it: I got my ass kicked," adding, "but I'm still happy, and I'm still dreaming." He decided to take a gap year before matriculating at Claremont—a school with a fiercely independent ethos that Ben's counselor thought would be a good fit.

This is where Ben's story becomes relevant to our quest to understand underscheduling. He wrote on his blog that one of his life principles is "to expose myself to bulk positive randomness." He made few plans for his gap year beyond booking plane tickets to various international destinations. His goal was to keep his itinerary open, encounter as many interesting things as possible, and then follow up on whatever caught his attention. In other words, he was going to travel the world living the underscheduled life.

He tempered his expectations for the trip, casting it more as a time of relaxation and contemplation, but underneath those careful words was the thought that perhaps something big might come out of his underscheduled walkabout. As he wrote right before leaving, "Who knows . . . maybe I'll move a mountain."

If you had asked him then to predict the events that would unfold during the year to follow, he would never have guessed just how effective his strategy would prove.

A Fateful Decision

Two days after receiving his high school diploma, Ben left for the first leg of his gap-year travels: a seven-week tour of Europe.

He eventually wandered into a quiet suburb of Zurich, Switzerland, where he visited the family he had stayed with during a summer spent as a high school exchange student.

"I was doing so much reading while traveling," Ben recalls. "I was reading, and writing blog posts, and sending these long e-mails describing my trip, and it got me thinking a lot about writing." This saturation in writing sparked an interest in Ben, which motivated him to dig deeper. (As the law of underscheduling states that when something catches your attention, you should always follow up and see where it leads.)

"I started e-mailing publishing contacts," Ben recalls. Most of his e-mails were a dead end—he received rejection notices from more than a dozen publishers and agents—but one resulted in a promising lead. "Earlier, this reporter wrote an article about me and my company. I had kept in touch with him, and now, when I wrote him, I asked if he knew anyone in publishing. He gave me a name. I followed up. That person passed me on to someone else at Wiley. I tracked the second person down, and he said, 'You can send me something.' "

Fortunately, Ben had something to send. Over the past several years he had kept a journal about his dual life as a teenager and an entrepreneur. He recorded his thoughts because he thought "it might be cool to look back on this time later in my life." But now these private thoughts had a public role to play. Ben put the file on disk. It was, as he describes it, "a big-ass Word document" of seventy thousand to eighty thousand words. He was leaving the following day for the next leg of his trip, so he asked his host family if they would print the file and mail it to his contact.

This is a classic example of underscheduling at work. When an interesting idea occurs, you should immediately follow up. Ben had a sudden interest in writing, so he took action by contacting the appropriate people in his network. Many might get this far, but then abandon the cause when the next steps become murky and difficult. Not Ben. His first round of e-mails generated a lot of dead ends, but eventually his persistence turned up a single new lead. Undeterred, he followed up on this lead, and the leads it generated, passing from one person to another until he landed at someone willing to look at some writing. As he was about to discover, his persistence would pay off.

When Ben returned to California, he had a message waiting from the editor at Wiley. The editor wanted Ben to sign a contract and transform the thoughts into a book right away— before his gap year ended. Ben had just enough time to sign the contract before leaving for the next leg of his gap-year travels, a month in Japan. He soon found himself in a position he could have never imagined on his graduation day four months earlier. He was holed up in a cramped hotel room in Kyoto, frantically editing the manuscript for his first book.

"I had eighty thousand words and I had to cut it down significantly. I was Skyping with my editor every night."

Two weeks later, he moved on to Hiroshima, where he finished his first draft. He e-mailed a copy to his dad and asked him to print it and send copies to Ben's mentors for feedback.

Indispensable to this step in Ben's rise to superstar status is the flexibility afforded by underscheduling. If Ben had filled his gap year with an ambitious schedule of activities and obligations, he wouldn't have been able to make such a radical shift and devote so much time to an unanticipated project. But with an open schedule, he was able to say, without reservation: "Let's go for it."

The effort paid off. After some more back-and-forth with his editor, and advice from his mentors, the manuscript was massaged into the final form that would become the memoir *My Start-up Life*.

Reflecting on the experience, Ben can't help but be amazed. "I knew nothing about the publishing process," he told me. "It all happened because I kept in touch with some reporter in case one day I needed some advice about his world. I definitely didn't set aside six months of my life to write a book."

From Print to Radio and Beyond

Ben wasn't done. In six short months he had gone from a standard student vagabond on a European tour to an absurdly young author. In true underscheduling fashion, however, he refused to stop there. He leveraged his newfound credibility to expose himself to new, even more interesting sources of positive randomness.

With book promotion on his mind, Ben called the public relations department at Claremont. He wanted to see if they had any contacts that might prove useful. (Sense a pattern? Part of Ben's approach to exposing himself to positive randomness is the relentless contacting of people who might lead somewhere interesting.) Ben chatted with a publicist, who was impressed with both the book and Ben's boldness in calling. The publicist made some calls on Ben's behalf. One of the calls went to a friend who happened to be an editor for *Marketplace*, an NPR program produced in Los Angeles and syndicated to 490 stations nationwide.

"The timing was perfect," Ben recalls. "It was back-to-school week on the show, so they commissioned a commentary from me on how college students could think like an entrepreneur"—one of the main ideas in Ben's upcoming book. This was serendipity, for sure, but it never would have happened without Ben's active efforts to make potentially serendipitous contacts.

As usual, Ben jumped at the opportunity. He wrote his essay, got feedback from people he trusted, and in general took the time required to make it as good as possible. The producers accepted the clip. Once this entrée was established, Ben began pitching new pieces, following the underscheduling dictum that once something proves interesting you should follow up aggressively.

Some of his pitches were rejected, but a few were accepted. The program's editors eventually made him a regular commentator, allowing him to speak on a variety of topics.

Ben had no master plan for becoming an NPR commentator. He was just performing the standard underscheduling shuffle: expose and follow up, expose and follow up. Or, as Ben modestly puts it: "One thing led to another."

Once Ben had the book and the NPR slot, his exploration began to yield new opportunities at a furious rate. He contacted anyone he had ever met who was affiliated with a university and tried to arrange a time to come speak about his book. This coalesced into a speaking tour that dominated the final months of his gap year. The meager speaking fees added up to enough to cover travel expenses, and he was soon crisscrossing the country, forming relationships with influential academics and business personalities. The tour even allowed him to fulfill a "long-dreamed-about goal": after a speech at the University of Arizona, he spent a night in the Grand Canyon. During this period, Ben spent a few months helping out a prominent venture capitalist in Boulder, Colorado, which, in turn, ratcheted up his connections in the world of entrepreneurship.

By the time Ben arrived at Claremont, in the fall of 2008, his story was radically different from that of the young student who had graduated from high school fifteen months earlier. At that point he had been a bright kid with mixed grades who once ran a Web company. He was now an author, radio personality, popular speaker, and well-known business pundit. The Politics Online portal named him one of the twenty-five most influential people in the world of Internet and politics, and the *Silicon Valley / San Jose Business Journal* named his blog one of the top twenty-five in Silicon Valley. When the organizers of the Claremont gala needed to select a handful of students to represent the school, choosing Ben was a no-brainer.

Looking back on this frenzied period, Ben concludes: "This all happened because I had these months free of commitments." His experiment with underscheduling proved an unequivocal success. No amount of careful planning or ambitious scheduling could have matched the levels of interestingness generated by the simple strategy of keeping an open schedule, exploring things that seem interesting, and persistently following up on every cool opportunity.

For Ben, underscheduling worked phenomenally well and phenomenally fast. This gives hope that if you use the advice in the upcoming playbook to systematically expose yourself to the world, your transformation may follow a similarly speedy trajectory.

5

The Underscheduled Student

IN 2007, a college counselor named Pam Proctor published a guide titled *The College Hook*. The book promised to help students develop a "hook" to differentiate themselves from the great masses of overachievers applying to the same schools. Proctor uses a cooking metaphor to describe this strategy—hooks are something you "cook up" according to a "recipe." Her approach asks the student to list the "ingredients" he or she has on hand— that is, the student's interests and accomplishments. The student then uses the list to choose the best match from one of the ten "hook" recipes described in the book, including the "International Hook," the "Technology Hook," and the "Music Hook." Next, the student plans a bold action to strengthen his or her connection to the hook. For example, if you like computers, and therefore decide that you fall into the Technology bin, Proctor suggests "creating a computer service organization to help senior citizens."

Pick up almost any guide on the admissions shelf and you'll read some variation on this strategy, which I summarize as:

1. Identify something that interests you.
2. Devise an impressive activity that proves your commitment
   to the interest.

I've noticed that this approach dominates popular thinking
about how to boost your admissions chances. Many high school
students, for example, have sent me an e-mail that follows this
basic format:

> **Hi, Cal! I'm trying to look more interesting to colleges.
> I guess I've always liked** [*name of some activity that the stu-*
> *dent has some interest in*], **so would it be impressive to the
> admissions officers if I** [*vague, unoriginal plan involving the*
> *activity—usually starting a club dedicated to it*]**?**

One young man, for example, told me that he liked Ping-Pong
and wondered if starting a Ping-Pong club at his high school
would increase his chances of cracking the Ivy League.

It doesn't take an admissions guru to see the problem with this
approach: it produces unoriginal, contrived, and fake-sounding
accomplishments. These watered-down, counselor-inspired "hooks"
are so common that I've taken to calling them *prefab*. When students sit down with their parents or counselors and try to master-
mind an extracurricular strategy, they invariably default to one of
the same small number of bland formulas. The resulting prefab
hooks bore admissions officers to tears. For example:

* You started a club around your hobby? *Prefab!*
* You signed up for a summer program at your local
  university? *Prefab!*
* You spent a month on an international mission trip that
  accepts anyone whose check clears? *Prefab!*

Here's the important point: I've never met a relaxed superstar who planned the sources of his or her interestingness in advance. (There was certainly nothing prefab or preplanned about the eventual accomplishments of Olivia, Jessica, or Ben.) This is the crucial distinction that separates the life of an underscheduled student from that of the average student looking to boost his or her admissions chances. The former lets interestingness form naturally from an interesting life, while the latter tries—and almost always fails—to force it all at once.

With this in mind, let's revisit the wording of the law that motivated Part 1:

The Law of Underscheduling
Pack your schedule with free time. Use this time to explore.

The lifestyle generated by this advice follows a different rhythm. Forget trying to identify your interest in advance. The under-scheduled student enjoys free time—*abundant* free time—in her schedule. She doesn't fill every minute with the heaviest course load conceivable or the uninspired activities chosen to support a prefab hook. She instead experiences the rare pleasure of having more than enough time to handle her work exception-ally well, while still leaving many hours free to relax. She takes advantage of this freedom to explore—exposing herself to as many potentially interesting ideas and opportunities as possible, looking for that one serendipitous match that will blossom into a deep interest.

"I wasn't stressed like the other students at my school, because I wasn't interested in trying to impress colleges," Olivia told me. "I still don't understand how I got into UVA. I find myself to be the luckiest person in the world."

It's a nice life.

I hope that I've convinced you that underscheduling yields more benefits than trying to think up prefab hooks or suffering through the conventional strategy of showing commitment to as many things as possible. I must admit, however, that the details of making the underscheduled lifestyle real are nontrivial. Two practical questions plague those who follow this approach. First, how do you inject free time into your schedule without simply quitting everything and looking like a slacker? Second, how do you effectively "explore" in this free time without having it degenerate into a morass of TV watching and Web surfing? In the playbook that follows, I will walk you through specific strategies to avoid both of these pitfalls, and to successfully integrate underscheduling into your student life.

Part 1

Playbook

THE HIGH-LEVEL concepts behind the law of underscheduling are simple. By keeping an open schedule and using your free time to explore, you maximize your chances of developing deep interests. The powerful trait of interestingness, in turn, can be generated *only* by these deep interests. And interestingness will make you shine in the admissions process.

As mentioned, however, putting the law into practice can prove complicated. For example, you have to decide *how much* free time is enough, and what it actually means to "explore interesting things." This playbook addresses these issues with specific advice. For clarity, I've divided it into two sections. The first section focuses on how to *simplify* your schedule. It covers topics from planning your workday to reducing the time demands of your course load. The second section tackles how to *explore* interesting things. The advice ranges from the power of developing a reading habit to techniques for soliciting guidance from experts in fascinating fields.

As always, my advice is meant to provide a starting point

for your experiments with the underscheduled lifestyle, but it's hardly the last word on the subject. Use it to build your momentum, but then please, by all means, break away from my suggestions and begin to experiment with different strategies to see what fits your personality best.

Simplify

The Ideal Student Workweek

The law of underscheduling says that you should leave *significant* amounts of free time in your schedule. But how much time is enough? From my experience, there's no magic number of commitments. In Part 3 of this book, for example, you'll meet a relaxed superstar named Maneesh who had periods in high school when he was a member of a large number of clubs. You might think this would have overwhelmed his schedule—but it didn't. When you dig deeper, it turns out that he would usually attend club meetings held during the school day but, as a general rule, skip anything scheduled after 3 p.m. The point is that a large number of clubs didn't add a large time commitment. Tons of students, like Maneesh, bounce in and out of a variety of minor activities—usually for social reasons—without suffering from time famine. However, I've also met plenty of students who were overwhelmed by a single demanding commitment (editing a school newspaper, for example, is famously soul-sucking).

My point here is that activity counts are meaningless, so forget, for now, how *many* things you do. Let's talk instead about what your day should *feel* like, regardless of your specific commitments. With this in mind, I have some straightforward advice for achieving a properly underscheduled lifestyle: embrace the *student workday*.

The concept works as follows: Every day you have a clearly

identified cutoff point in the afternoon or evening that signifies that you are absolutely, nonnegotiably, done with work. The hours after this cutoff point are free for you to do whatever you want. Once you're done for the day, you're really done. This time is 100 percent unstructured and unscheduled—the type of time the law of underscheduling demands for exploration.

There are two big advantages to a student workday. First, it clearly segregates free time from work time. This sounds self-evident, but I want to emphasize that it's a huge deal. Too many students mix these together, letting their evening slosh past as a slurry of halfhearted work and aimless Internet walkabouts. To get the true benefits of free time—the mental unwinding that releases stress—the time has to be completely, unapologetically free. By hunkering down after school, getting your meetings and work done, and then saying, "I am now free to do whatever I want," you'll enjoy a profound boost to your happiness. This time, of course, is also when you can deploy the deep-interest-producing exploration that you'll learn about in the second section of this playbook.

Clear segregation of your time is just the first advantage. The second argument for embracing a student workday is that it sharpens your attention. When you're racing toward a cutoff point, you're more likely to focus on your work—actually concentrating on getting it done instead of succumbing to the half-working, half-distracted state that I call *pseudowork*. This focus generates better results and reduces the time required for completion by a ridiculous amount—a double whammy of goodness.

However, we're still missing a piece to the puzzle. The idea of a clear end point for the day is good—but where should this end point be located? This varies depending on the student and the workload. But for the sake of extracting the most advantage out of an underscheduled lifestyle, I'm going to give you an ambitious target:

The Ideal Student Workweek
During a normal week, your work should be done by dinner-time on weekdays and require one half day on either Saturday or Sunday, but not both.

Right now, this might sound crazy. I should first clarify that by "normal" I mean a week that doesn't have an unusual workload, due, for example, to preparing for upcoming exams or the SAT, or whatever. But even allowing for these exceptions, you're probably still confounded by my optimism.

I understand.

The thought that you'll be able to finish your work by dinnertime may sound unrealistic. But have faith. In the playbook subsections that follow, I'm going to walk you through a series of specific strategies for reducing the time required by your schoolwork. You'll learn the secrets of efficient studiers. I'll pitch the idea that you should study at the local library. I'll try to convince you that Facebook is the tool of the devil. And you'll learn how to finish a surprisingly large amount of work in school before the final bell rings.

For many students, however, more efficient work habits won't be enough to make the ideal student workweek a reality. They simply have too many hard courses and too many time-consuming extracurriculars. The only solution here is to do some quitting. This prospect can be scary, but the final subsections of this section of the playbook will introduce you to what I call *the art of quitting*, smart advice for reducing what's on your plate in a responsible way.

Many of the relaxed superstars you've met, or will meet later in this book, were able to achieve this ideal student workweek. I'm confident that once armed with the advice that follows, you can do the same.

How to Reduce Your Homework Time by 75 Percent

Professional swim coach Wayne Goldsmith once noted an interesting phenomenon about world-class swimmers: when major record holders were asked to reflect on their record-breaking races, they were almost always surprised by their performance. Penny Heyns, for example, a former record holder in both the 100-meter and 200-meter breaststroke, recalled the following about her races: "When I touched the wall, I thought, maybe a 2:30, and this felt too easy for that. . . . I really don't know what happened." (Penny's time of 2:23.64 set a women's Olympic record for the 200-meter breaststroke in 1999. The record held until 2001. The current record is 2:20.22.)

According to Wayne, this reaction is more the rule than the exception. As he explains, in swimming, speed is different from effort. Any athletic person can jump into a pool and swim a lap as hard as possible. The swimmer would expend a huge amount of effort—most of it in the form of splashing—but is not likely to move all that fast. Speed, on the other hand, comes from technique: a perfect stroke rotation, a flawless kick-turn, a dive into the pool with no unnecessary drag. When swimmers break world records, it's because they achieved perfect technique during the race. They are, of course, still expending serious effort, but they're not completely draining their batteries. Too much juice and their technique might become sloppy; the speed gained by better technique dwarfs what's gained by simply swimming harder.

This is why swimmers are often surprised by how relaxed they feel during their best performances. Breaking a major record in this sport has nothing to do with pushing the body past its limit. It is, instead, dependent on finding that Zen rhythm, where all of the swimmer's carefully calibrated skills deploy with synchronous efficiency.

Students can learn a lot from the insights of Wayne Goldsmith, because with studying, like swimming, technique trumps effort. Imagine two students studying for a math exam. Assume the first student studies for five hours and deploys the standard high school strategy of haphazardly reading through the textbook and randomly tackling sample problems. The second student studies for two hours and has better technique. Let's say she's built a detailed study guide that she reviews by trying to explain complicated concepts and answers to problems out loud, as if lecturing an imaginary class, instead of just silently reading to herself.

From my experience, the second student will score at least as well as the first student, and likely even better, even though she spent less time. In both cases, technique trumps effort. Like the record-breaking swimmer, our second student will finish the test and think, "That wasn't so bad," while the first will be exhausted by the effort and probably frustrated with the outcome.

This example captures the secret behind how you can drastically reduce the hours you dedicate to homework. By teaching you better technique, I'll enable you to maintain your grades (or perhaps even improve them) while spending much less time. This is, of course, a crucial step toward achieving the ideal student workweek without coming across as a slacker.

Let's get started. Below, I describe a collection of simple ideas about your academic work habits. Some may sound like common sense, and some may surprise you, but they're all tested, and they've worked time and again in real classrooms. Put this advice into action and you'll be surprised by how little time you actually need to keep up with a high school workload.*

---

* For more detailed studying advice, I also recommend taking a look at my book *How to Become a Straight-A Student*. It's written for college students, but many high school students have reported great success in adapting its ideas to their situation.

Technique 1: Be Organized

For each class, keep a college-ruled notebook and a stack of plain manila folders. Take all of your notes for this class in the notebook. For each test or paper in the class, label a fresh folder for holding the materials you need. For a test, the folder might hold old exams and study guides. For a paper, it might hold your research material and rough drafts. You'll probably need an administrative folder for holding general information about the class—handouts describing assignment due dates, etc. The general rule, however, says that every piece of paper you get in the classroom goes either into the trash or into a labeled folder—no exceptions.

This is all you need for your organization system: a notebook and a pile of labeled folders for each class. It's simple, but it will save you significant amounts of time spent scrambling to find what you're looking for. It also builds a foundation of confidence—"I'm in control"—that makes it easier to adopt the more advanced techniques that follow.

Technique 2: Let Your Notes Do the Heavy Lifting

On the teenager-boredom scale, most students rate note taking slightly below watching an all-day marathon of *The PBS News-Hour*. The result is shoddy, halfhearted, chicken-scratched notes that aren't very useful. When it comes to studying for a test, most students are then forced to invest an absurd amount of time in trying to track down the relevant information and reformat it so that it can actually be understood. It's this *relearning* of information that makes studying such a mind-melting chore. It's also a huge waste of time.

When it comes to notes, the secret to saving time is straightforward. If you actually invest the mental energy required to learn the information when it's first presented, and then capture this learned information in an easy-to-review format, you'll find that the time needed later to prepare for the test will be drastically reduced.

Here are some tips for taking notes that live up to this standard:

DON'T SIMPLY TRANSCRIBE THE FACTS SPEWED OUT BY THE TEACHER OR PRESENTED IN THE TEXTBOOK. Instead, try to organize the information into *big ideas*. One approach is to use the QEC (question/evidence/conclusion) method, which, as I described in *How to Become a Straight-A Student,* is popular among high-scoring college undergraduates. The method is simple: Reduce the information presented to you into *questions* paired with *conclusions*. Between the two, list the evidence that justifies the connection. In other words, the questions and the conclusions become a wrapper around the raw facts—transforming them into self-contained ideas.

Let's try an example. Imagine you're in an AP U.S. history class, and your teacher is discussing the signing of the Mayflower Compact. Most students would simply try to write down everything; e.g.:

* The compact was signed in 1620 off the coast of Cape Cod.
* It described the system of representative government to be followed by the colonists.
* It ### [indecipherable chicken scratch].

The QEC method, by contrast, forces you to consider what's important about this information—not just copy it down. Notes in this format start with the question posed by the information. In the AP U.S. history example, your *question* might be:

* QUESTION: Why was the Mayflower Compact important?

As the teacher continues, record the relevant facts below the question—these will form the *evidence*. They'll look like our bullet points from above ("The compact was signed in 1620," etc.). You're not off the hook yet. As you record this evidence, begin thinking about what *conclusion* the teacher is pointing you toward. Review your evidence as it grows; keep thinking. Eventually, a conclusion will hit you. In our example, it might read something like:

* CONCLUSION: The Mayflower Compact established representational government as an important feature of the American colonies. This was different than the monarchies that controlled European countries. It helped lay the foundation for our current democracy.

Sometimes you won't be able to come up with a good conclusion in the heat of the moment. That's okay. In this case, write the word "CONCLUSION" in your notes and then leave the next couple of lines blank. At the end of class, go back, look over the evidence, and try to fill in the empty spots. If you're still stuck, ask your teacher for help. Trust me, a student coming up after class to ask an insightful question is what teachers live for.

These exact same ideas apply to the reading assignments you do at home. As you pore through your textbook, take your notes in the QEC format. If you get stuck on a conclusion during homework, try rereading the introduction and conclusion of the relevant chapter. Often you'll find high-level analysis tucked in these bookend sections. If you're still stuck, mark this place in your notes with a question mark and ask your teacher about it the next day. Whatever you do, don't simply highlight your textbook—this does nothing to help you learn the information.

The QEC technique saves time because it forces you to process the information as it's presented. Later, when you come back to study, you're just reminding yourself of big ideas you've already learned. This is much faster than silently reviewing facts and hoping that you can come up with interesting conclusions from scratch during the test. Students who process the big ideas early end up studying less later, and scoring higher.

FOR MATH COURSES, RECORD SAMPLE PROBLEMS AND EXPLANA-TIONS.   As the teacher walks your class through a sample problem on the chalkboard, record the question, the answer, and the intermediate steps in your notes. If she moves too fast for you to capture all of the steps, still make sure you get the question and answer down, so you can use them to practice later.

The best math students also take notes on the teacher's explanations. For example, when the geometry teacher describes a strategy for deciding which rules to use for estimating angles, don't tune her out while waiting for the next sample problem to begin. Instead, take notes on her big-picture explanation. Math teachers invest a lot of effort into figuring out how to explain the ideas behind the techniques they teach. Take advantage of this reality by recording these ideas. Don't just record them verbatim, however, as this allows you to escape real understanding. Instead, rewrite them in your own words.

In general, when it comes to math notes, be bold with your formatting. I've seen students draw big arrows from explanatory text to steps in sample problems. I've also seen them sketch big stars next to important ideas and add little notes to themselves in the middle of a solution. This is all great. The more you engage with the material, and try to understand it, the better.

FOR DISCRETE POINTS OF INFORMATION THAT HAVE TO BE MEMORIZED—E.G., NAMES, DATES—RECORD THEM ON INDEX CARDS.   Put a question on one side of the card (e.g., "What year did Japan bomb Pearl Harbor?") and the answer on the other side

("1941"). It's okay to bring index cards to class and jot down the prompts as the teacher mentions them (this saves a step later). Do the same while reading your textbook—transfer facts to be memorized straight onto the cards. To study this information, shuffle the deck and try to answer the question on each card. Put the cards that stump you into a separate pile and return to them later. There's nothing new about flashcards, but many students bypass them out of laziness. Don't do this! They're the fastest way to memorize facts.

IF YOU HAVE TO MEMORIZE LABELS ON A DIAGRAM—E.G., THE PARTS OF A CELL FOR BIOLOGY CLASS—MAKE SEVERAL PHOTOCOP-IES OF THE DIAGRAM WITH THE LABELS COVERED OVER. The best way to learn diagrams is to try to fill in blanked-out labels and then check the original to see how close you came to getting it right. Once you're able to re-create all of the labels from scratch, you're done. Don't get frustrated; as with the flashcards, this style of *active recall* takes time until the information seems to sink in. But once it sinks in, you're not going to forget it.

IF YOU DON'T UNDERSTAND SOMETHING IN CLASS OR IN A READ-ING ASSIGNMENT, PUT A SERIES OF BIG QUESTION MARKS IN YOUR NOTES TO CLEARLY IDENTIFY THE TROUBLE SPOT. Your goal should be to replace the question marks with the right infor-mation within *forty-eight hours*. There are three approaches to achieving this goal. You can go back and reread the relevant sec-tion of the textbook. You can ask the teacher. Or you can see if Google has some advice on the topic. (It's surprising how often reading a different take on the same subject can help you under-stand the original text better. This is especially true for math, where sites like MathWorld and Wikipedia have clear explana-tions for most math concepts—from geometry to multivariable calculus.)

From my research on study habits, I've learned that a large amount of time spent studying is devoted to tracking down answers to these tricky questions the day before the test. If you make a habit of eliminating your confusion as it arises, you'll find that the studying process goes much faster.

All of the tips on note taking presented here aim you toward the same goal: ensuring that by the time you start studying, you've already completed most of the hard work of grappling with and conceptualizing the information covered on the test. As you approach test dates, I don't want you to have to waste a single minute trying to make sense of your notes—you should face only the much easier process of reviewing things you already understand.

So now that you have the notes down, let's learn how to study.

Technique 3: Reject Rote Review

We've discussed the stuff that happens *before* you begin studying. Now we'll tackle the dreaded chore itself. My philosophy is founded on the following belief: The absolute worst way to study is to reread your textbook and notes silently to yourself. I call this flawed technique *rote review*. It's how most high school students study, and it requires an incredible amount of time but produces only mediocre results.

By contrast, the fastest way to review material is to engage in *active recall*. This technique has you explain the relevant ideas out loud, without peeking at your notes, as if lecturing an imaginary class. If you can explain a concept in full, articulate sentences, then you can be sure of two things: first, that you understand it, and, second, that you won't forget it. As with most of the techniques described in this section of the playbook, active recall requires more mental energy than the alternative.

But in exchange, it allows you to learn the material better and in much less time.

Here are some tips for applying the active-recall approach to different types of material:

* **Non-math Courses.** If you followed my earlier advice, you've taken notes in the QEC format. As promised, this simplifies the studying you now face. Each big idea cluster—consisting of a question, evidence, and a conclusion—is a separate entity to be studied. To do so, cover the evidence and conclusion and read the question. Next, try to recall the conclusion and a collection of the evidence that connects it to the question. (You don't have to recall every last piece of evidence—just enough to make a compelling argument is sufficient.) This recall should be completed *out loud*: speak in full and articulate sentences, as if lecturing a class. If you get through the recall of a cluster without major stumbles, then you're done studying that concept. Don't bother returning. If you have trouble, review your notes and then mark the troublesome cluster to return to later, after the information has left your short-term memory. Don't skip the out-loud piece of this technique. If you don't speak it, you won't learn it!

* **Math Courses.** To apply active recall to math, you should attempt to re-create the steps and answers to the sample problems recorded in your notes. You should also walk through the high-level explanations you captured (if you followed my note-taking advice, you wrote down these explanations as the teacher gave them). Don't peek at your notes during this process. If you can't recall what's important without help, then the idea has not yet stuck. Here's the crucial point: as with the non-math courses, you should narrate this review out loud. When doing sample problems, pretend

you're presenting them on the chalkboard—narrating every step along the way. The same goes for the high-level explanations. You should see if you can explain them from memory, as if addressing bored students. Without the narration, you're in danger of simply memorizing the solutions without understanding the underlying concepts—a habit that will come back to haunt you when you're faced with new problems on the test.

* **Memorized Information.** Some information, such as dates, names, and labels for diagrams, has to be straight-up memorized—there are no big ideas or complicated explanations to narrate. If you recall, I suggested that you record this information on flashcards or on diagrams with blanked-out labels. There's no shortcut to learning such information beyond working with these aids until you stop making mistakes. The good news is that this process is more mindless than the active review described above, so you can do it in small batches at random times. My main advice for this style of studying is to avoid leaving it until the last minute. Memorizing is tiring! If you're forced to do it for hours the night before a test, you'll suffer, and probably end up not learning the material all that well. A smarter approach is to start way early—maybe two to three weeks before a test—with memorization. Spend ten to fifteen minutes with your flashcards, a few times a week, as the semester progresses. You can even do this between classes or while waiting to be picked up from school. These many small sessions add up to save you a lot of painful work at the end.

Technique 4: Write Papers over Three Days

High school students hate writing papers. More than they should. If you think about it objectively, writing a paper should seem preferable to studying for a test. There's no need to learn complicated ideas or memorize facts, and there's no worry about facing a new problem, with five minutes remaining until the bell, and suddenly realizing that you have no idea how to solve it.

A paper is written on your own terms. You're given weeks to formulate your ideas and construct something worthwhile. If you don't understand something, you can look it up. Need a break, take one. Yes, paper writing should be seen as a treat. But, of course, it's not.

The reason for this paradox is obvious: students don't start writing papers early enough, and they end up trying to cram it all into one night, which is a terrible and painful experience. This is why students hate papers—not because they're intrinsically hard, but because the way they tackle them is stupid.

It's easy to just say "Start earlier," but this rarely solves the problem by itself. When you ask yourself the vague question "Should I start today?" the answer is almost always "Nah." Every day seems busy, and without a specific schedule that you trust as making sense, procrastination will usually win out.

I want to free you from such a fate with a concrete approach to scheduling your paper writing. It can be stated as follows: If you want to write good papers without stress, use three days. The first day should be for researching. This is when you go back through the novel you read, and/or your notes from class, and figure out what you're going to say. Capture this in a simple outline. (The format of the outline doesn't really matter; what's important is the thinking behind it.) If possible, after you finish your first draft of the outline, go do something else, preferably something relaxing. After you've cleared your head, return to your thinking fresh and see where you can make it better. This can make the difference between a passable paper and an exceptional one.

Most students mash together the thinking and writing pro-
cesses, figuring out what they want to say as they're saying it.
This leads to rambling, semi-incoherent papers, and makes the
whole process more painful than it needs to be. You can sidestep
this whole morass by isolating the thinking to its own day. Once
you're done with your outline, stop.

The second day is for writing. Using the outline from the
research day, scratch out a decent draft of your paper. Don't
worry about careful editing. This day is about getting your argument into reasonably crafted words. When you finish this draft,
as before, stop for the day.

The third and final day is for editing. I usually recommend at
least two passes. You can do the first pass on your computer. Look
for obvious mistakes, and fix your structure and transitions. In
general, make the paper read like a good paper. When you finish,
it will still have small mistakes, but its overall shape will be solid.
For the second pass, print out a draft and read it out loud. This
is the fastest way to root out the remaining small issues. If you
skip using your voice, and insist on reading silently to yourself,
you *will* miss things. One out-loud pass is better (and faster) than
multiple silent read-throughs.

You need at least one full night's rest between each of these
three days. The days don't, however, have to be consecutive. It's
fine, for example, to research a week before the due date, and
then write and edit in the final two days. What you cannot do is
combine any of the days. This holds even if the paper is short and
requires only a couple of hours from start to finish—keep the sep-
aration intact. By doing so, you'll not only significantly improve
the quality of your work, but you'll also make it significantly
less painful. Better yet, this approach reduces the impact of the
paper on your schedule. Doing an hour or two of work each day,
over three days, makes it possible to maintain your ideal student

workweek. By contrast, an all-night marathon is brutal and can bust your attempts to enforce a consistent work cutoff point.

"But wait!" you cry. "I'm too much of a procrastinator to start three days early! I can *only* do the work with a deadline looming."

I must respond to this common reaction with some tough love: *Suck it up.* If your goal is to succeed in competitive college admissions, you're going to have to embrace some self-control. I'm not asking you to be rigidly disciplined. Instead, I'm asking that you add just a *little* more structure to your process. The good news is that the urge to procrastinate diminishes when your mind actually trusts that your schedule makes sense. The three-day rule works, and your mind will believe this. The result is that you'll require less willpower than you might have feared to stick with the plan.

Now let's tackle our final technique for easing your homework requirements.

Technique 5: Study like Darwin

The note-taking, studying, and paper-writing techniques I described above really work. I've observed dozens—if not hundreds—of students find success with these approaches. They shouldn't be, however, the final word on the subject. Every student is a little different, and every class presents its own unique demands. With this in mind, perhaps the most important piece of advice I can give you is to always be experimenting and improving your own personal set of study habits.

After every test or paper, put aside a few minutes to perform a short postmortem on the experience. Ask yourself the following questions:

* What preparation helped me?
* What preparation didn't help me?

    ✹ What could I have done, but didn't, that would have made a
       big difference?

I don't mean this in the vague sense that you should give some
general thought to your performance. I want you to literally ask
and answer these three specific questions after every major test
and paper you face as a high school student.

    Next, use your answers to the first three questions to craft
your response to this fourth and most important prompt:

    ✹ How am I going to prepare for the next test or paper?

This five-minute process will yield huge benefits for your studying
techniques. Over time, your skills as a student will evolve to better match your unique personality and work demands. If you're
jealous of those lucky students who seem to do very well without burning the midnight oil, you can be sure that they didn't
stumble into a smarter way of studying; they probably evolved it,
through trial and error, using a process like the one above. Follow
their lead and never settle for your current flawed habits. If you're
always improving, your work times will continue to plummet.

Facebook Is the Tool of the Devil

My local library got me into Dartmouth. To be more specific, I
mean an isolated row of study carrels, stacked against a window-
less wall across from the magazine racks. This library, you should
understand, occupied a small lot next to the midsized, central
New Jersey public high school I attended. This made it easy for
me to visit after school, without having to make a special trip. In
the fall of my senior year, when it came time to study for the SAT,
I took full advantage of the proximity of this ideal study location.

The thing about preparing for the SAT is that taking practice tests is hard. My mind has a way of wandering when faced with a difficult chore. This proves especially true, as I discovered around this time, when you're in a household with multiple screaming siblings and every other imaginable distraction.

"That's enough for today" was the inevitable declaration that signaled that I had once again succumbed to temptation.

This sad state of affairs led me to the library's study carrels. Once I was there, something about the silence and the idea that I was far from home and its distractions, in a place that served no purpose other than being a quiet spot to work, focused my attention. I could concentrate like a monk when sitting alone back by those lonely racks of magazines. And this concentration helped me master the art of taking the SAT. The resulting high score put schools like Dartmouth on my admissions radar. (Recall, as I explained in the "Common Questions" section, that the first step to college acceptance is getting your grades and scores above the minimum threshold for your reach school. Only then can the relaxed superstar lifestyle work its magic.)

I became so enthralled by the concentration generated at the library that I began to do more of my schoolwork in its quiet recesses. The effect was profound. When I would arrive at the library and say, "I am going to work for the next two hours, then go home," I could accomplish a sizable amount of work. By contrast, if I spent two hours "working" at home, ten feet from an Internet connection and a flight of stairs away from a TV, my work amount plummeted.

This brings me to the following crucial point: Your environment plays a *huge* role in how well and how long you do your schoolwork. If you're careful about when, where, and for how long you study, you'll experience a significant reduction in the time required to do good work. Here are some basic work rules:

Rule 1: Work in Isolation

Find your own equivalent of my isolated library carrel. It should be a location that's silent and separated from easy distractions. Don't choose somewhere near your home or where your friends regularly congregate. It should be enough of a pain to get from this location to anywhere interesting that you're likely to actually stick with your work until you're done.

Rule 2: Work in Fifty-Minute Chunks Followed by Ten-Minute Breaks

Break up your work into hour-long chunks. Focus during the first fifty minutes of the hour, and then take a break for ten minutes. Once the break is done, immediately start your next chunk. You can tweak these amounts to better suit your own energy rhythms, but I've found that the fifty/ten split almost always works best for students. After about three hours of this rhythm you need a longer break; make it somewhere between twenty minutes and a half hour. (Fortunately, if you follow all of the advice in this playbook, you should rarely need more than two or three of these chunks on any given day, so these long breaks may be unnecessary.)

Rule 3: Get as Much Work Done in School as Possible

When interviewing underscheduled students for Part 1 of this book, I was surprised by the amount of schoolwork they were able to accomplish during the school day. On further reflection, I saw that this strategy makes a lot of sense. For one thing, during the school day you don't have the possibility of stopping to watch TV or go online, so you concentrate more easily. Underscheduled students take advantage of this forced concentration to whip through homework fast. You may protest that you're already busy during the school day, but experience has taught me that most students do have quite a bit of free time sprinkled throughout their schedule—they just need to know where to look. For example, several of the underscheduled students I interviewed accomplished a lot of their math or science homework during class. As the teacher explains Lewis structures on the chalkboard in chemistry class, you can immediately be putting that knowledge to work, while it's still fresh in your mind, to make progress on the related homework problems. Similarly, if you have a study hall period, forget idle gossip and go to the library to get stuff done. And so on. Once you activate the mind-set that you're trying to squeeze work into every free slice of the school day, you'll be surprised by how much actually gets accomplished.

Rule 4: Avoid State-Transition Cues

A *state-transition cue* is any activity that shifts your mind-set from high-intensity concentration to low-energy relaxation. Checking your Facebook feed is a state-transition cue—your mind has jettisoned its focused work mind-set for the low-energy search for easy stimulation. Turning on the TV, checking e-mail, or texting a friend are also state-transition cues.

As you might imagine, once such a transition occurs, it becomes very difficult to return to work—and the work you do manage to do will be slow, inefficient, and sloppy. In recognition of this danger, foster an obsession for avoiding these cues—like a vampire shunning garlic—until your student workday is complete. After this workday is done, of course, go nuts. But before then, be on your guard.

Going straight from school to an isolated study location, of the type described in rule 1, is an easy way to steer clear of these transitions. Setting simple and clear rules also helps. You might declare absolutely no Internet until after dinner, or disable the text message notifications on your cell phone until after you get home. If you don't own a car, you can use this situation to your advantage. Find an isolated location that is walkable from your school, but not from your home, and then arrange to be picked up by a parent right before dinner—perhaps on his or her way back from work. This physically prevents you from encountering most transition cues; you're stuck in an isolated study location, so you might as well study. Once you know your enemy (in this case, the transition cues), it is much easier to defeat it.

Rule 5: Keep Your Energy Levels Stoked

If your physical energy gets low, studying becomes a dreary chore. So be vigilant about keeping yourself fed. After school you should be eating something that provides good energy once every hour or so. The simplest rule for choosing these snacks is to avoid anything that comes in a plastic bag or wrapper. Such items aren't really food; they're just fancy-looking mashes of corn syrup and artificial flavoring, and they will make you crash. Anything with protein (e.g., peanut butter, cheese, yogurt), or anything unchanged from its natural state (e.g., fruit), will give you longer-lasting energy. I don't care about your Doritos craving. You can eat crap when your student workday is over. During the heat of battle, you need every ounce of concentration you can muster.

Rule 6: Do Not, under Any Circumstances, Do Any Work Anywhere Near an Internet Connection

In rule 4, I described going online as a common state-transition cue that should be avoided until after the student workday is completed. This point is so important, however, that I'm giving it a rule to itself. I don't want there to be any ambiguity here, so let me be clear: *Do not do* any *work while online.* If you're writing a paper, or working on math problems, or taking notes on your history textbook, with an instant messenger window open, there's absolutely no way that you can realize the ideal student workweek. The work done in this state is poor, it is draining, and it takes forever. If you work while online, you *will* end up staying up late, you *will* end up doing shoddy work, and you *will* fail to achieve an underscheduled lifestyle—and therefore lose all the benefits that this lifestyle generates.

This rule is so important that I sometimes advise parents to physically remove the cable connecting the computer to the modem until their kids are done with their homework for the day. If the student needs to do research for a paper, parents and student can agree on an exact time frame in which this research will be done and the parents can reconnect the cable for only this period.

When it comes to productivity, there's no avoiding this truth: Facebook is the tool of the devil. If you want to significantly reduce the time you spend working, then you absolutely have to keep the Internet far, far away until you're completely done for the day.

Time Management for Students Who Have No Interest in Time Management

When I advise college undergraduates, I spend a lot of time discussing time management. These students face demanding commitments, from rigorous academic work to joblike clubs. Because of this reality, I offer them a mature collection of tools, referenced by the decidedly unsexy name Getting Things Done for College Students (or GTDCS, as my most hard-core readers like to call it). They have in-boxes, calendars, next-action lists, and complicated project rules. It's not easy, but for many of these college students, it's crucial.

Fortunately, high school students don't need anywhere near this level of complexity to manage their time, especially if they're living an underscheduled life. The high school workload is easy and predictable enough to make such intricate planning unnecessary. However, if you let your schedule flap completely loose in the erratic winds of your work responsibilities, you're often going to be dragged into trouble. Assignment deadlines will sneak up and collide, and you'll be forced to scramble, maybe late into the night, to get everything done. This will happen again and again. You'll hate it, and it'll destroy your attempts to maintain the ideal student workweek. With this in mind, I suggest a simple technique that will help you avoid such a fate.

I'll start with the underlying concept. The key to avoiding work pileups, not surprising, is to spread out your work. If you need five focused hours to study for a biology test, divide the task over a few days to avoid having to keep five full hours free on any one night. In general, if you break big projects into lots of small chunks, it becomes much less likely that too many time requirements will accumulate on a single day.

This idea is straightforward, but a lot of students will still balk, claiming that they're constitutionally incapable of starting work early. They will then utter, in hushed tones, their fear of "procrastination." Let me demystify this fear once and for all. Most procrastination comes from bad work habits. If you study haphazardly, in big, painful rote-review sessions, never quite sure what you should be doing or for how long, your mind *will* revolt and try to stop you. On the other hand, if you follow the advice given earlier in this playbook, and apply smart review techniques in focused locations with high energy levels, you will reduce the procrastination urge to something you can conquer.

The challenge that remains is constructing the plans for how you'll spread out your work. You cannot rely on a spontaneous decision to start work early on a long-term project. Tomorrow will always seem like a better day than today, and you'll end up waiting until the day before. What you need is a concrete schedule, constructed in advance, that spells out exactly which days you're supposed to be working on each big assignment, and what you'll be doing during those days. You can then blindly follow this plan—avoiding the need to fight the daily mental battle generated by asking yourself: "Should I work today?"

This brings me to the simple time-management technique I promised in the heading above. Here's what I want you to do: Buy a large calendar and place it somewhere where you'll see it. I recommend the fridge, as this makes your work commitments public. If your mom knows you're supposed to get started on your paper the Sunday before it's due, you'll gain two immediate benefits: (1) she'll be impressed by your studiousness and therefore be more lenient where it counts, and (2) you'll be more likely to actually do the work, because if you don't, you'll have to face the inevitable questions about why you're ignoring your schedule.

Once you've set up your calendar, use it to record the due date of every major test, paper, and assignment. This ensures that you'll see, every day, in plain black ink, what deadlines are looming. Never again will due dates sneak up on you.

You're not done yet. The second piece to this technique is to follow what I call *the two-week method*. Each evening, right before dinner, take a look at your calendar. Find the current date, then jump ahead two weeks. For each deadline on this future date, you need to construct a plan for how you'll complete the corresponding work. First, make a rough estimate of what steps are needed and how long each will take. Break this work into a collection of reasonable-sized chunks—perhaps one to two hours each—that can fit easily into your student workday. Next, schedule the chunks on *specific* days on your calendar—actually write them down on those days.

Imagine, for example, that you look at your calendar and see that a history exam is two weeks away. It's time to create a plan. You might decide that you need around two hours to catch up on the final reading assignments, another three hours to do active-recall review on the big ideas captured in your notes, and around an hour to memorize the dates on your flashcards. It adds up to six hours of studying time. You might then break this amount up into three chunks, each around two hours. Let's assume that the test is on a Friday. Furthermore, let's assume that, during the week of the test, you have a track meet on Monday and plans with a friend on Thursday. Noticing these existing commitments, you might schedule the first chunk on the Sunday before the test, the second on Tuesday, and the third on Wednesday.

To make things more interesting, let's assume that you also have an English essay due that same Friday. Once again, you shift into planning mode. Using the three-day paper-writing rule presented earlier in this playbook, you know that you need three chunks of time: one for research, one for writing, and one for editing. Because the paper is short, one hour each for the first and third chunks, and two hours for the second, will suffice. Looking at your schedule, you notice that your free time is rapidly diminishing. Let's assume that in addition to your test studying on Tuesday, you have to tackle your weekly math homework on that night as well. You fear that adding work on the paper to this day would make the pile too high. With this in mind, you move back another week in your schedule, and put your research chunk on that Thursday. This is pretty far in advance, but your calendar made it clear that time was too limited to fit all three chunks into the week before. You might then put your writing chunk on Sunday, and the editing chunk on the Wednesday before the deadline. (Notice, I didn't consider Friday, as it's always nice to keep this night free.)

Once you see the plans in plain ink on your calendar, they seem like an obvious way to break up the work on those projects. And they are. But without the calendar, you would *never* have stumbled into this schedule. There was no way that a week before a paper deadline, for example, you'd suddenly think: "Maybe I should start working on my outline today." The calendar captures the reality of the work landscape you face, and helps you navigate an efficient and low-stress path through it. This simple tool, coupled with the two-week method, will keep your student workday intact, even through the busiest of periods.

When All Else Fails . . . Quit

I've just taken you through a lot of advice on study habits, procrastination defusing, and time management, along with comparisons of a certain social network to the devil (which will likely earn me fun letters from the more religious among you). My hope is that this advice proves sufficient to streamline your current schedule to fit inside the ideal student workweek. If, however, you're the type of student who lobbied your school for permission to squeeze in an extra hour of AP classes during your lunch period—the type of student who views extracurricular activities as a volume business—then calendars and isolated study carrels won't be enough. The advice will help, but it won't get you down to the ideal schedule. To accomplish this final goal, you must wield the underscheduling weapon of last resort: *quitting*.

Fear not, I won't ask you to haphazardly hack and slash your commitments down to an unimpressive pile of slackerish nothing. There's a fine art to quitting without reducing your perceived impressiveness. In the next two subsections, I'll introduce you to this art. Coupled with the smart work habits already described, it will enable you to get to the underscheduled lifestyle you need to enter the world of the relaxed superstar.

The Art of Quitting, Part 1: The Final-Straw Effect

I'll begin by focusing on your course load. In an age in which many students consider the number of AP courses they take as a key metric for college admissions, it's common for homework alone to be enough to bust your ideal student workweek—even if you have smart work habits. If this is the case for you, then your only option is to reduce your course burden.

When considering your schedule, divide your courses into three categories: showboat, required, and elective. *Showboat* courses are your most impressive offerings. Depending on your ability, they might be AP courses, or they might be honors-level courses. Regardless, they're the most rigorous subjects you're taking and they're important for establishing a high level of academic rigor on your college application. By contrast, *required* courses are those you have to take because they satisfy some requirement you need for graduation. You may not care much about them, but they're there because they have to be. Finally, *elective* courses are those that are not particularly competitive—you choose them, mainly, because they seem fun, and to fill the remaining free slots in your schedule. These might include an English course dedicated to Shakespeare or something more technical in nature, like architecture.

The question you face is how to take this collection of courses and reduce it down to something less time demanding. Fortunately, the right answer doesn't usually include a *drastic* reduction to the number and difficulty of your subjects. The more common experience is that a student's academic schedule is fine until he adds those extra courses that destabilize the whole thing. Those final courses become the straw that breaks the camel's back—taking a schedule that was stable and manageable and pushing it into a stressful, time-consuming mess. I call this *the Final-Straw Effect*, and knowing about it is good news for you, as it means that you don't have to take a hacksaw to your courses to gain some relief—a carefully wielded scalpel will serve instead.

For example, imagine a student named Charlie. Assume he's eager to gain acceptance to the Ivy League, and he believes that having his guidance counselor check that all-important "toughest course schedule available" box on his application is crucial to his goal. This leads him to pack as much as possible into his course load. For his showboat courses, he's planning on taking AP English, AP European history, AP biology, and AP chemistry. For his required course, he's taking geometry. For his electives, he's signed up for art history and computer science. Add gym and lunch to the mix, and that's one full schedule.

Charlie knows that a similar schedule proved overwhelming during the previous semester. Even with efficient work habits, he was often up late, struggling to keep pace with his assignments. He wants to know what to cut before the next semester begins.

He doesn't need drastic reductions. His problem comes from having one or two hard courses too many—creating just enough work to ensure that deadlines frequently collide and pile up, and to transform any missed day into a disaster that necessitates late-night catch-ups.

Charlie's first step is to remove his single most time-demanding showboat course. The removal of one such course won't change an admissions officer's perception of his academic rigor, but it can significantly reduce his stress. For Charlie, this thinking leads him to kick AP chemistry off the island—hearing horror stories of long lab write-ups and complicated exams has caused him to rank this course as the most demanding of his showboats.

Summary of step 1: **If you foresee that your upcoming course schedule will be too demanding, your first move should be to jettison the scariest of your showboat courses.**

Returning to Charlie, let's assume that he still needs more time reductions. His required course is there for a reason and cannot be lost, so the next place to look is his electives. Here's the great thing about these courses: they're hiding in the shadow of their showboat brethren—so no one will notice what you do with them. You can take advantage of this reality to gain significant time reductions without making your course load appear less rigorous. Assume, for example, that Charlie's art history course has a reputation as a silent killer—memorizing all those dates, he heard, takes forever. Because electives fly under the radar, he confidently drops the course and replaces it with a study hall. Not only does this remove a big time sinkhole from his schedule, but it adds forty-five new minutes during school each day to get a head start on his work for other courses. The total gains, therefore, are huge.

Summary of step 2: **The more you reduce the time demands of your electives, the easier your life will become, without decreasing the perceived toughness of your schedule.**

To simplify the process of reducing the demands of your electives, you should keep two things in mind. First, as in Charlie's example, don't hesitate to replace an elective you're ambivalent about with a study hall. A study hall adds a *negative* amount of work to your schedule by providing extra time to reduce the load generated by other classes. Ambitious students sometimes fear that taking study halls will mark them as not being the type of hyperdiligent masochist they think impresses admissions officers. *Forget this fear.* Your showboat courses indicate that you can handle a college-level course load. No one cares whether or not you took that pottery elective.

My second suggestion about electives is to be wary of *silent killers*. A silent killer, also as in Charlie's example, is a course that seems nonrigorous but ends up generating a huge amount of work. I've met students who had to dedicate many late nights to finishing sketches for a drawing course, or getting the glue to dry cleanly on a model for an architecture elective. These courses can deep-six your schedule with little to offer in return. Avoid them at all costs.

In the end, Charlie's final schedule seems just as impressive as his original schedule. But by dropping the hardest showboat course and replacing a silent-killer elective with a study hall, he has significantly reduced the demands on his time. This is the beauty of the Final-Straw Effect: you can gain huge benefits from nearly unnoticeable changes.

I'll conclude with a final big-picture warning. *Always allow genuine interest to trump the rules I've just presented.* If you're excited about a course, you should stick with it. As I emphasized earlier, authentic engagement is the fuel of interestingness. This doesn't give you permission, however, to maintain an unreasonable schedule. Instead, take your favorite courses out of consideration when you start cutting.

The Art of Quitting, Part 2: The Activity Andy Test

Now that you've lightened the demands of your course load, it's time to examine the other side of the student work coin: your extracurricular activities. If you still haven't achieved the ideal student workweek, even with efficient habits and an intelligently reduced course schedule, your extracurricular activities are the next logical place to start making some serious cuts. Don't be nervous about these reductions. Many students labor under the belief that surviving an overwhelming activity load, like surviving a killer course load, is a mark of ability and commitment that impresses admissions officers. This belief is flawed. Remember Olivia and Jessica: their extracurricular schedules were negligible, yet they still breezed into their reach schools. Their secret was interestingness, which trumped hardness and busyness during the admissions process. The path toward interestingness, however, requires an open schedule, so it's time to say goodbye to your position as secretary for the French club. I'm about to teach you how to underschedule your extracurricular life.

Imagine a student. He's plain vanilla through and through. He's not dumb, but he's not particularly bright either. His grades are fine, but not great. He's generally a happy guy, but not all that ambitious. I'll call this unremarkable soul Activity Andy.

Now consider your own list of extracurricular activities. For each activity, ask yourself the following question: *Is this something Activity Andy could do?*

It's a simple query, but it touches the core of what makes some activities worth it and some a waste of time. Any club that requires only that you show up and invest a certain number of hours, for example, is something Activity Andy could do. Ditto for any activity that's open to anyone who can pay. Examples of such Andy-friendly commitments include becoming vice president of the French club, attending a summer program for high school students at a nearby university (i.e., a money mill that feeds on students' college admissions ambition), going on an expensive, prepackaged international mission trip, or being a non-officer member on the student newspaper or yearbook staff.

Activity Andy could do any of these things. They require a reasonable investment of time. Some require money. But there's nothing about them that requires any particular sparkle of creativity or any real drive. There's no whiff of innovation or hint that the student is curious about the world. They'll all glaze the eyes of admissions officers and serve mainly to make your life more difficult. In fact, as you'll learn in Part 2 of this book, participating in too many of these activities can actually make you appear *less* impressive to the outside world.

For all these reasons, I want you to consider dropping every activity that Activity Andy could do. (If he could do it, then why would anyone care that you could too?) If you're worried that dropping an activity halfway through your school career will make you seem uncommitted, then leave the activity off of your college application altogether. *I'm serious.* This book is going to teach you how to do things that matter. Leave those lightweight commitments to your anxious and boring peers.

The small number of activities that *do* pass this test probably require a talent you've developed over time, or a spark of originality that Activity Andy would never possess. If you're a soccer star or a talented violin player, for example, then keep these pursuits. The same goes for the Web site design business you've launched, or the local comic book club you grew into a serious organization. Activity Andy would be confounded by such talent-driven or original actions, so they're good to stay. The rest, however, should go.

I should hasten to mention that there are two exceptions to observe in applying this test. You should always feel free to keep an Activity Andy–friendly activity on your list if it meets one of the following two criteria. The first is if it's something that requires only a small time investment on your part and that you joined for social reasons—say, to hang out with your friends or impress cute girls or boys. Without friends and flirting, high school wouldn't be high school.

A good example of this exception was my longtime membership in the model UN club. This commitment required a one-hour meeting, after school, once a week. There was also a conference, once a year, held at a hotel, which required a few nights of extra preparation. I joined this club because many of my friends did as well, and we wanted to spend a weekend together in a hotel, causing all sorts of badass model-UN-style mischief, focused mainly on trying to impress the cute representative from Libya. Sure, Activity Andy could have also joined model UN—the only criterion was showing up for meetings—and I don't think I even listed it on my college applications. But much more important, during my final conference in senior year, I actually convinced a girl I met there to briefly date me—making the entire endeavor worthwhile. I wouldn't want you to miss out on a similar victory.

The second exception applies to activities that align with your core values. If you volunteer at church, for example, because it's a community that is important to your life, then of course forget the Activity Andy test and keep volunteering. If you're doing it only because you think it shows character on your application, however, the exception doesn't apply.

In general, be wary. I mention these exceptions so that you won't remove things that are important to you outside the realm of college admissions. But don't go nuts. Your aim is still to achieve the ideal student workweek, so try to limit the number of activities that don't meet the Activity Andy test.

When the dust has settled, don't freak out. Your activity list may now look empty and forlorn, but this is a necessary starting point if you are to achieve the full power of the underscheduled lifestyle. Your next step is to use this newfound free time to explore—uncovering the deep interests that will, in turn, generate the interestingness that can make you a standout. The second section of this playbook describes strategies for exploration.

Explore

In early January 2009, I wrote a blog post titled "Start Your Semester Off Right by Quitting Something." It was a plea for underscheduling. I hoped to harness my readers' New Year–inspired self-improvement zeal to remove some time sinkholes from their schedules, and thereby lower their stress and help them open themselves to more potential deep interests. This was not the first time I had preached this message on my blog, and most students were happy for the reminder. But a reader named Kara was not.

"I have to disagree," she began. "Last semester I was very underscheduled and spent a lot of time just hanging out with friends. . . . Advocating more and more free, unstructured play-time does not work . . . for me. My brain operates best on a busy but balanced schedule."

Another student, Phillip, added that if he reduced his work

time, his attention would simply transfer to all of the leisure activities competing for it: "sports, video games, TV, friends, and food."

And a student who went by the pseudonym "supergirl" seconded these concerns by admitting: "I dropped lots of things last semester and just spent an embarrassing amount of time online."

This trio of dissenters highlights an important point. Many students fear, and rightly so, that if they reduce the stuff in their schedule, they'll just fill their new free time with laziness—decreasing their impressiveness. As another student reacting to this post put it, there's an "inertia" built from busyness that keeps him rolling through the work that he hopes will eventually get him into college. Clearing out his schedule, he noted, would act like a brake on his forward progress.

Fortunately, the law of underscheduling addresses this concern. While the first half asks that you leave significant amounts of free time in your schedule, the second half adds that you should use this time to explore. It's this exploration clause that will save you from a descent into laziness. If you can direct the free time toward exposure to interesting things, you'll develop deep interests. The deep interests will then generate interestingness, which will make you much more impressive than the overscheduled drones you're competing against for admissions slots.

There is still the question of how to best inject such exploration into your life. The goal of the remaining sections of this playbook is to describe specific strategies for doing so. These strategies will help you transform the ideal student workday into a powerful, deep-interest-attracting magnet.

Cultivating a Reading Habit

I can teach you the secret to scoring in the high 700s on the verbal section of the SAT. In fact, I can isolate a *single* trait shared by every high scorer on this section whom I've ever met. These students started reading adult-level books around the third or fourth grade.

Memorizing vocabulary lists can improve your verbal score. But the students getting 780s and above are lifelong, precocious readers. I was one of those students. I read my first real novel, Michael Crichton's *Jurassic Park,* in the third grade. By the time I entered my senior year of high school, the verbal section of the SAT was a breeze. Reading-comprehension questions seemed straightforward, vocabulary words familiar; even the words that I couldn't precisely define still emanated some essence of their meaning. The word "loquacious" might baffle the average seventeen-year-old, but to a reader, even one who doesn't know its exact meaning, its correct definition ("full of excessive talk") will somehow just seem *more right* than the other options. (A lifelong reader has probably encountered the word enough times in books that some sense of its meaning is buried deep in the folds of his or her brain.)

The benefits of this habit, however, extend far beyond SAT scores. Lifelong readers also write better. Through sheer exposure to prose, their sentence structures gain complexity and rhythm. When reviewing e-mails from the students who follow my blog, I can easily sort the readers from the nonreaders. Consider the following two sentences, each taken from a different student e-mail currently in my in-box:

* "Certainly, I was devastated by the whole thing, but now I realize that it may have been a blessing in disguise."
* "I recently stumbled upon your Study Hacks blog and I was mulling whether you will create a post about increasing

> vocabulary by any chance because I know it is the
> foundation of good essays."

It doesn't take a professional grammarian to deduce that the first sentence came from a serious reader. (Even more impressive, the student who wrote that e-mail is only a freshman in high school—perhaps a budding relaxed superstar?)

Lifelong readers are also better able to focus on complex ideas, and this helps them in a variety of academic situations. In a column that appeared in the *New York Times* on July 4, 2009, Nicholas Kristof noted that American children who stop reading over summer vacation actually lose IQ points due to the lack of mental exercise.

"A mountain of research points to a central lesson," Kristof wrote. "Pry your kids away from the keyboard and the television this summer, and get them reading."

Put simply, for students, reading acts as a wonder drug.

The reason I mention this habit here, however, is that it also provides a powerful catalyst for the development of deep interests. Reflecting on my own life, I notice that almost every major deep interest driving my student career owes something to books. In high school, I cofounded a small technology company, Princeton Web Solutions, with my good friend Michael Simmons. The superficial interest I'd had in entrepreneurship became deep enough for me to launch this venture only after I read Stephen Manes and Paul Andrews's biography of Bill Gates. When I arrived at college, I settled on a computer science major because I thought it would support a career in start-up business. But after reading several scientist biographies, notably James Gleick's *Genius: The Life and Mind of Richard Feynman* and Sylvia Nasar's *A Beautiful Mind: The Life of Mathematical Genius and Nobel Laureate John Nash*, I developed a deep interest in math and theory that propelled me into the PhD program at MIT.

My compulsive reading habit bathed me in potentially interesting information. After years of this exposure, a few things remained with me long enough to become deep interests—and these changed my life.

The general observation here is that reading is an excellent vehicle for the exploration piece of the law of underscheduling. Cultivating this habit is one of the most important things you can do with the time we freed up in the first section of this playbook.

Some students worry, however, that an obsession with reading is a trait you're either born with or not. Here's my stance: There's no such thing as a natural-born reader. Just because you don't read a lot now doesn't mean that you're missing some key gene. Students become "natural" readers due to environment and luck. Perhaps, when they were growing up, they happened to have access to lots of books, or they came across a title exciting enough to propel them into reading more complicated prose. When I was eight, for example, the thrill of dinosaurs devouring paleontologists was enough to drive me through my first novel, even though much of it escaped my understanding. The point here is that there's no magic to becoming a reader. Some are lucky enough to stumble into this category, but there's nothing to stop you from getting there by choice. In this section, I'll teach you how to do it.

Let's start with a common pitfall. Something I've noticed when advising students to start reading is that they believe they should be tackling big, important books. For example, in response to an article I wrote on this topic, a student named Ian wrote me for some book recommendations. He told me that he had been trying to work his way through "Hemingway, Steinbeck, Faulkner, and Fitzgerald" but was falling short.

There's nothing wrong with reading the great authors. But I think the idea that only the canonical texts count keeps a lot of young people away from the shelves. Ian was struggling with these books, and his struggle was preventing him from developing a reading addiction. So I'll throw caution to the wind and say it out loud: *Screw the canonical texts!* The key to cultivating a strong reading habit is to find books that keep you up late at night reading—whatever they are. They don't have to be novels. Indeed, one of the fastest ways of building the habit is to take a topic you already love—baseball, *Star Trek*, business—and find nonfiction books about it. Reading doesn't have to be an exercise in self-control where you work through a "good" book because you've been told a thousand times that it will change your life. Search instead for something that captivates you. For your goal of exposing yourself to interesting ideas, it doesn't matter whether or not the book won a Booker Prize.

With this caveat in mind, I have two specific pieces of advice for getting started down the road to reading. First, make a trek to Barnes & Noble, or a similar book megastore. Go alone and give yourself plenty of time. Start browsing the tables of new releases. Seek out sections that match some interest you already have. (Seriously, anything you're interested in has a book written about it somewhere in that store.) Build up a pile of books that pique your curiosity. Remember: Screw quality! Interest rules in this exercise.

Next, take your pile to the in-store café. Buy a coffee. Settle in and start reading. When I'm doing a session of this type, I proceed one book at a time. I start by reading the description and the blurbs on the jacket, trying to get a feel for what the book is about and why it's supposedly important. I'll then usually read the introduction and skim through some promising chapters to get a sense of the main ideas. In most cases, I then move on to the next book. If the book really happens to catch my attention, however, I may ignore the rest of the stack and really start reading. I may even go home with the book. I'd estimate that 10 percent of the books I pick up really capture my attention.

This approach is all about exposure. The megastores have a huge selection, and the books are arranged on tables and in shelf end-cap displays to catch your attention. In such an environment, you can quickly gain a sense of exactly which types of books really do hold your attention. These are where you should start.

I suggest making an expedition of this type at least once a month. If you're rolling in money, you can actually bring home your favorite find after each expedition. For most of us, however, this is impractical—which brings me to my second piece of advice: Use your local library. Regardless of the size of your local library, it is undoubtedly plugged into a network of many more branches. If, during one of your bookstore expeditions, you encounter a book you love, you can then request it from your library network. The network will deliver it to your local branch for you to pick up and read for free. If no one else has requested the book, it will arrive in a day or two. If there is a long waiting list, it could take weeks. The key is to continually add books that catch your attention to your request queue. This ensures a steady arrival of titles at your local branch.

It's this one-two punch—frequent browsing at a big bookstore plus requesting the most interesting books from your library—that can knock you into a serious and addictive reading habit. Try this approach for just a few months, and you'll be surprised by how interested you become in the printed word. What's more, this exposure will become one of your most important sources of deep interest.

The Saturday-Morning Project

In my first book, *How to Win at College*, I introduced the concept of the Grand Project, which I described as follows:

A Grand Project is any project that when explained to
someone for the first time is likely to elicit a response of
"wow!"

Examples of such projects include:

* Writing a screenplay
* Trying to get a short story published
* Launching a microbusiness
* Mastering an interesting and unusual hobby
* Building a popular blog
* Starting an activist movement

In *How to Win at College*, I advised all students to launch a
Grand Project, and I offered two main rationales. First, these
projects inject excitement and possibility into your life, thus
helping to keep you optimistic through the small ups and downs
of the standard student experience—a bad grade, a lost boyfriend,
etc. It is the second reason, however, that's most relevant to our
discussion here about exploration. I noted that Grand Projects
have a way of attracting other random and cool opportunities.
Once you start down the path to building a popular blog, or fir-
ing up a student activist movement, you throw open the door to
what Ben Casnocha, mentioned earlier in Part 1, called "bulk
positive randomness." In other words, choose a Grand Project
because it sounds exciting and will keep your life interesting, but
be ready for it to potentially introduce you to a deep interest you
had never before considered.

You may object that this scheme could cause a conflict. Projects require time and commitment. The law of underscheduling,
by contrast, wants you to *reduce* your committed time. This is
where the "Saturday-Morning" piece of this subsection's title

comes into play. A Saturday-Morning Project is a Grand Project with one important addition: you work on the project only on Saturday morning, between the time when you wake up and lunch. What's cool about a Saturday-Morning Project (or SMP, for short) is that you gain the two benefits of a Grand Project (excitement and exposure to cool things) without introducing a major time sinkhole into your schedule. Saturday morning is rarely filled with other obligations, so you're making use of time that would otherwise lie fallow to make consistent progress on something interesting. Of course, if an SMP takes off, you can increase the time you dedicate to it. But if you're lucky enough to get to this point, then the project has probably transformed into a true deep interest, so you can feel comfortable making it one of the small number of things you seriously focus on during the week. Above all, keeping an SMP alive will strengthen the ambitious and confident mind-set necessary for the type of aggressive exploration that makes the law of underscheduling work.

Join Communities

In the introduction to this book, I mentioned Kara, a student from the Bay Area who got accepted into Stanford and MIT, even though she had Bs on her transcript and a sparse extracurricular schedule. In Part 3, I'll tell the full story of Kara's remarkable admissions coup, explaining exactly how she got involved in the activities that made her a star. But in this chapter, I want to give you a preview. Specifically, I want to highlight an important component in her improbable rise: *community*.

As a sophomore in high school, Kara, along with a couple of friends, began volunteering at a local community center. The center assigned her to a project that required the videotaping of World War II veterans, to capture their memories of the war. Most weekends that year, Kara and her friends would dutifully lug a video camera to yet another ranch house or bungalow tucked away on some sunny California street, set up the tripod and boom microphone, and then walk the subject through a list of questions.

At this point, there was nothing spectacular about Kara's involvement. There was no deep interest; it was just a volunteer gig with her friends.

But then things changed. One weekend morning, after setting up her camera and asking the first of the standard questions from her list, she realized that her subject was someone special. His natural timing and rich baritone made the interview compelling, and his experiences were unique and infused with insight. Kara edited the interview and showed it to her supervisor. He also thought it was special, and he invited Kara to present the clip at a fund-raiser for the center. This raised her profile within the organization. The executive director, impressed by her professionalism and interest, asked her, "What would you like to work on next?" Kara had a bold suggestion involving the construction of a new health curriculum. (One of the center's other projects was developing technology-based curricula for school.) He told her to do some more research and then get back to him.

As mentioned, you'll encounter the full story of what happened next in Part 3. What's important to know for this chapter is that two years later, by the time Kara's college counselor was balking at the lack of AP courses and club memberships on her application, Kara's curriculum idea had developed at an astonishing pace—eventually being adopted by schools in ten states. At the core of this exceptional accomplishment was community. Without a community to channel her energy and provide structure and resources for her project, Kara would not have been accepted into Stanford and MIT. As I'll argue below, joining a community is one of the most important things you can do to foster deep interests and then nurture the projects they inspire.

I'll start with the basics. When I say "community," I mean

any group of individuals who work together toward a common cause. Communities exist both offline and online. The fans that run the sprawling Lostpedia Web site for ABC's hit series *Lost*, for example, form an online community. The community center where Kara volunteered was an offline community. In Boston, to give another example, there's a group of skeptics who meet most weeks to share a drink and talk science. This is a wonderfully nerdy gathering. It's also a community. As is the group of film buffs who meet every Sunday morning at the historic, single-screen cinema on Brattle Street in Cambridge, Massachusetts, to screen independent films making the festival rounds.

Communities act like interestingness incubators. If you join a community, you'll immediately encounter a variety of small projects you can adopt, and little actions you can take to advance them. These small steps generate larger and more exciting opportunities. The community gathers these opportunities, combines them with the resources and support needed to realize them, and then doles them out to its members as they're earned.

Kara benefited from this reality. The community center, with its many members and charismatic founders, attracted a lot of grant money and was engaged in a variety of projects. When Kara joined, she was immediately exposed to small things she could do to help—for example, filming veterans. As she paid her dues on these initial projects, she gained access to larger projects already under way within her community. When she began developing an idea for a health curriculum, the organization could offer her a large amount of support. When she needed to test her lesson plans in a classroom, the organization already had programs in place with the local school districts that could easily be repurposed to this cause. And when the curriculum eventually spread to ten states, it should be no surprise that these were ten states where the community service organization already had relationships with the school districts.

Put another way, Kara could never have come close to her final accomplishment if she had been working on her own. It was not raw brilliance or creativity that made this curriculum happen. It was the combination of her deep interest and hard work *with* all of the support, focus, and resources provided by her community.

This story of a community acting as an accelerant for an interesting person's rise to prominance is not rare. To give another, somewhat esoteric example, consider the massive and well-organized fan community surrounding the Harry Potter books. In 2001, a recently graduated college student named Melissa Anelli moved back home while searching for a job. She wanted to be a writer but didn't know where to get started. To ease the anxiety of her situation, she spent her spare hours posting on the message boards of a popular fan site called The Leaky Cauldron.

As Anelli recalls in her 2008 book, *Harry, a History*, a single event soon occurred that changed the course of her young life. It started when she broke a "major" story for the fan site. *Vanity Fair* was scheduled to release the first pictures from the set of the first Harry Potter movie. This was a big deal for Harry Potter fans, as it would provide a glimpse at how the world of Hogwarts would be portrayed on-screen. Melissa persuaded the corner-store grocer in her hometown to sell her a copy of the magazine a day before its official release. She scanned the photos and sent them to The Leaky Cauldron's editors, who promptly posted them. Within the community, it was considered a big score, driving lots of traffic to the site. That raised Melissa's profile. She began to track down more big stories. Among other victories, she was the first fan site writer to get the PR department at Warner Bros., which produces the Harry Potter films, to return her calls and confirm or deny rumors. Eventually she was promoted to Web mistress of the site, and then she took control of the entire enterprise when its founders moved on to other things.

As the fan community surrounding Harry Potter grew, so did the opportunities available for Melissa to act on her deepening interest in writing and reporting. She gained allies within the Warner Bros. studio and at Scholastic, the company that publishes the Harry Potter books. In perhaps her biggest victory, she interviewed and befriended the books' author, J. K. Rowling, herself—and Rowling recorded the opening to The Leaky Cauldron podcast. In 2008, when Anelli published *Harry, a History*, these connections, and the insider information they afforded her, helped propel the title onto the *New York Times* bestseller list.

Like Kara, Melissa needed a community to channel her energy. Without it, her determination to be a successful writer would probably not have led to the bestseller list. The community made it possible.

Here's my advice for taking advantage of this power: If you have a casual interest in a topic, seek out and join a related community. Participate regularly in this community, using the abundant free time generated by the underscheduled lifestyle to jump at small projects and opportunities as they arise. At this early stage, follow-through is critical. Every story I've ever encountered about someone being catapulted to prominence involves that person not only volunteering to take on small projects but then also following through to completion—again and again. This is part of the reason why I had you free up so much time from your schedule, so you can tackle challenges like these as they come up, without an overbooked course load or too many boring extracurriculars draining your availability.

In summary, the secret to leveraging communities is simple: *Pay your dues, and bigger opportunities will arise.* Before you know it, the variety of fascinating, impressive projects available to you will grow. As with Kara and Melissa, getting involved with a community might prove to be the most important single step you take on your path to superstardom.

The Advice-Guide Method

In an essay titled "The Narrative Idea," written for the Nieman Foundation's annual conference on narrative journalism, the late author David Halberstam offered a powerful suggestion for young journalists:

> When you find a reporter whose work you admire, **break his or her code.** Examine the story and figure out what the reporter did, where he or she went, how that reporter constructed the story, and why it worked [emphasis mine].

At the core of this advice is a simple idea: *Blind effort, by itself, is worthless.* Plenty of people in the world work hard without reaping much reward for their effort. There are tens of thousands of aspiring writers, for example, who invest huge amounts of time in crafting a novel or pitching articles to magazines, yet still never get anywhere. I occasionally hear from students who tell me that they've spent the last year crafting a 100,000-word book, and they want me to connect them with an editor who'll publish it. I ask them if they've tried to sign with an agent (a necessary first step), or, for that matter, if they have any professional writing experience. The answer is invariably no, which, as it turns out, is the answer they then receive from publishers when they send an unsolicited copy of their "masterpiece." It's not that these students aren't capable of producing a good book, it's just that they didn't take the time to learn what's really involved in making this happen. They didn't crack the code of published writers.

This same logic, crafted by Halberstam for the writing world, can also apply to *any* casual interest that you want to transform into deep interest. Here's a common scenario: In the abundant free time generated by your underscheduled student workweek, you encounter something that piques your curiosity. Perhaps it came up in a book you read or is an opportunity that arose from a community you joined. After a few days pass, you notice that your excitement about this pursuit remains undiminished, so you decide to go after it seriously. What should you do next? Taking your cue from Halberstam, your best next step is to crack the code—that is, figure out exactly what it takes to succeed in this particular pursuit. By doing so, you'll gain two immediate advantages. First, this knowledge builds confidence that will help you stick with the pursuit during its transformation into a sustained deep interest. Second, you'll discover what next steps to take—a surprisingly difficult question to answer for many pursuits.

I call this approach the *advice-guide method*, because it asks you, in effect, to research an advice guide for succeeding in a field before you jump into action. If you're seeking real accomplishment, this is unquestionably the best way to proceed.

But how does one conduct this research? In his essay, Halberstam spelled out a method for cracking the code in the specific world of journalism. He suggested that you read the reporters you admire and then try to identify exactly what about their writing, as compared to that of other writers, impresses you. Below, I generalize this idea into a three-step process for accomplishing something similar in *any* field of interest:

1. Find examples of people who have succeeded in the field, and examples of people who *did not* succeed.
2. Compare the success stories with the failure stories and identify where they differ.
3. Contact one of the people who have succeeded and ask for specific advice.

These three steps capture the core idea behind Halberstam's advice: Ground yourself in real examples and real people. Unless you draw on specific examples, you run the risk of generalization or falling prey to popular but unsubstantiated myths. It's easy to come up with advice that sounds right. It's much harder to find advice that actually works. That's why you have to start with primary sources.

Consider the rapidly expanding world of blogging—an appealing pursuit for many students. Let's imagine that you're interested in growing a popular blog. If you ignore the advice-guide method, and instead search online for a few tips before diving into action, you risk accepting some of the false beliefs that permeate this field. You might decide, for example, that the key to success is a fancy Web site, or publishing lists of links that might attract a large number of Digg votes. But if you followed the advice-guide method, and worked with real examples and real people, you might choose a very different course.

In fact, while researching this topic, I decided to put the above claim to the test. Adopting the scenario described—a high school student looking to build a popular blog—I went through all three steps of the advice-guide method. Below, I report the results.

Step 1 asks that I find examples of successes and failures in my field. For my successful blog example, I used J. D. Roth's phenomenally popular Get Rich Slowly personal finance blog—dubbed GRS by its fans. JD has over 70,000 RSS subscribers and attracts over 750,000 monthly visitors. Running GRS is his (lucrative) full-time job.

For my failure example, I wanted something that tackled the same topic as GRS—personal finance—so that I could compare apples to apples. This was easy enough to find. I first did a Google search for "personal finance blogs"; then I scrolled to the dreck hidden deep down in the search results. I quickly stumbled across a typical mediocre blog—it had only a few readers and sporadic postings.

Step 2 of the advice-guide method asks that I compare the two examples to identify exactly what separates them. To keep

things fair, I decided to look only at the first two months of postings from each site (the amount of time before GRS became JD's
full-time job).

Here are the traits I noticed about GRS:

* JD posted almost every day during the first two months of
  the blog.
* The articles were professionally crafted and edited. JD
  would lay out his thesis, offer specific advice—usually
  accompanied by abundant links to related resources—and
  then conclude with a list of similar articles the reader might
  also enjoy.
* In his first week, JD covered the following, among other
  topics: how teens can better manage their money; how
  to decide whether to repair or junk an ailing car; the best
  online financial calculators; an innovative strategy for
  saving money; and traits shared by people who become
  millionaires. There were no musings about his weekends or
  apologies for slow posting.
* He introduced several regular series, such as "Pep Talk"
  and "Frugality in Practice," that focused on the topics of
  articles that his readers seemed to enjoy most.
* His advice was often unexpected. Almost every article
  included a new twist or an idea that went beyond common
  sense.

By contrast, here are the traits I noticed about the failed personal finance blog:

* Most of the advice was written in the first person and drew
  heavily on personal opinions. The style was informal and
  emoticons were used with distressing frequency.
* Only 30 percent of the posts focused on specific advice. The

rest were a mix of the author's reactions to other articles, personal notes (e.g., "I'm taking the weekend off," or "Here's a story about something interesting that happened to me"), and random links.

* The advice articles reeked of *mind dumping*; that is, they had the feel of an author just rattling off the first things that came to mind in order to have something to publish. A post on saving money at the grocery store became mired in generic and obvious tips, including: stock up on sale items, cook instead of buying prepared foods, and beware of the expense of organic food.

This comparison exercise, which took me less than an hour to complete, yielded tremendously useful insights about succeeding in the field of advice blogging. I learned, for example, that a successful advice blog requires that you focus almost exclusively on producing a regular series of advice posts, and avoid posts on your personal opinions or lists of random links. I also learned that advice is worthless unless it tells people something they couldn't have thought of on their own. And the advice should be presented in a professional style.

This covers the first two steps of the advice-guide method. The third and final step asks that you actually contact someone involved with a successful example of the pursuit, and then ask for guidance. This step is tricky. By definition, if the person is successful, he or she is probably busy and likely to ignore a rambling or unclear e-mail from some random high school kid. You have to be strategic in your approach.

Here's my advice for making this contact work:

* Send the person an e-mail. Explain that you're in high school and that you're interested in the person's field and looking for advice.

* Be very clear about your expectations. I recommend listing
  two or three short questions at the bottom of the e-mail.
  Ask if the person is willing to respond to these queries.
* Make your questions specific. Anything too general—"How
  do I succeed?"—will be ignored. It's easy to answer specific
  questions. It's hard to ponder general, unclear prompts.
* Be succinct. Try not to use more than a line or two
  before getting to your request. Don't waste two or three
  paragraphs explaining who you are and what your situation
  is—the person will skim this at best, and delete the
  message at worst.

With these points in mind, I crafted and sent the following
e-mail:

JD,

I'm a student and a huge fan of your sensible but often
unexpected personal finance advice.

I'm writing because I'm serious about building a quality blog
that covers similar issues but with a tight focus on my fellow
students. I'm a big believer in gathering data before jumping
into a new project, so I was hoping—perhaps quixotically—
that you might take pity on an eager young student and
provide a few words of insight in answer to the 3 questions at
the bottom of this e-mail.

Either way, thank you for you contributions to the world of
finance advice.

Best,
Cal

(1) What single factor do you think most helped GRS succeed
when so many other personal finance blogs do not?

(2) If you had to write a to-do list for a new blogger serious about investing the time required to build a large audience, what would the top two items be?

(3) What myth about succeeding in blogging do you think is most damaging?

Keep in mind, when I sent this e-mail, JD had no idea who I was. He thought I was just a high school student contacting him out of the blue. Later, when I interviewed JD about my experiment, he admitted that he gets a huge quantity of e-mail and has to ignore most of it. My message, however, survived this screening and generated the following reply within just a few hours:

Hi, Cal.

I'll do my best to answer your questions. Let me know if you need more info!

(1) What single factor do you think most helped GRS succeed when so many other personal finance blogs do not?

I work at it. I work *hard*. I think many people jump into blogging—not just pf [personal finance] blogging, but all blogging—and think it's going to be easy. They think it's no big deal to write a new article every week—or every day. They're wrong. Writing one article is like a sprint. Writing one article a day for years is like many marathons put back to back. To do this well is very difficult. I had lots of practice before I started GRS. I've been writing for the Web since 1997, and keeping a daily blog since 2001. I knew it would be hard work. I think that nearly any blog at which the author spends 60 hours a week will be successful. (Proviso: the author must be able to write marginally well and produce content that is interesting. But those two factors aside, I think hard work will always prevail.)

(2) If you had to write a to-do list for a new blogger serious about investing the time required to build a large audience, what would the top two items be?

1. Take a writing class. This is number one by a mile. Most bloggers are poor writers. I like to think that I'm a good writer, and I *still* take writing classes. There's always something to learn.

2. Read. Read about writing. Read about your subject. Read everything you can get your hands on. Be a sponge.

(3) What myth about succeeding in blogging do you think is most damaging?

I think it's a myth that a successful blog will always be profitable. This isn't the case. While it's certainly possible to make an excellent income through blogging, there are many people who work just as hard as I do who aren't able to do so. Blogs are not an easy road to riches any more than anything else.

Let me know if you need more info, or if you have follow-up questions.

If I was actually a high school student interested in starting a blog, JD has just provided me with some invaluable insider advice—the messages about hard work, how long success should take, and the importance of writing ability are unexpected and immensely useful. And he has concluded his e-mail with the magic line "Let me know if you need more info, or if you have follow-up questions." I have now moved into JD's circle of acquaintances, meaning I can send follow-up questions and expect answers as I pursue blogging success. This single well-crafted e-mail has provided me a huge leg up in my pursuit.

After receiving this reply from JD, I came clean—confessing to him the nature of my experiment. JD, fortunately, was amused. "I've used similar techniques myself to get responses from big names," he told me. "Malcolm Gladwell let me reprint a part of *Blink* on my site—because I asked. If you ask, you're ahead of ninety-nine percent of the population."

When I asked JD about how he sorts his own e-mail and decides which to reply to and which to delete, he revealed that he replied to my test message because it was short and looked easy to answer—"I try to answer messages I think will be quick." But he still noted, "Yours was actually a *little* too long." For this busy blogger, his ideal message has "just a few sentences before the questions." Brevity is king!

Reflecting on this experiment, I realized that the advice-guide method provides an incredible head start for the pursuit of an interest. In less than two hours, I was able to use the method to generate targeted insight about building a successful blog. I learned exactly what types of posts work, and what types do not; received specific suggestions from an expert in the field; and also received an open offer to contact this expert with follow-up questions. I've encountered dozens of students who started blogs only to quickly abandon them after losing faith that they'd ever succeed. On one hand, if they had had the advice I'd obtained by applying the advice-guide method, not only would they have gained the confidence to persist, but they would have had a good chance of growing a big audience. On the other hand, they might have been dissuaded from continuing with the pursuit. (JD makes it clear that success does not come easily in this field.) But that could also be a useful outcome, as it might save them the time they'd waste discovering this for themselves over six months of bad posts and no visitors.

Blogging was just an example I chose to test the method in

action. The same results can be generated for almost any interest. When I decided to look into book writing, for example, I spent time comparing the top sellers to the flops in my topic area. I then tapped my contact network to set up a phone conversation with an author and a literary agent to get their expert advice on the crafting of a good book pitch. The fact that the book you're holding is my third shows how effective the method can be.

The advice-guide method works. It might require a little more time up front, but it helps you maximize your chances that a passing interest will turn into an impressive, accomplishment-generating deep interest.

Go to Interesting Places, Meet Interesting People, Stay in Touch

Earlier in Part 1, I told the story of Ben Casnocha's gap year. His commitment to underscheduling and exploration generated a book deal, an NPR commentator gig, and a speaking tour—all within fifteen months. But what happened after he arrived at college?

"I would say I went to twenty speakers per semester," he told me when I asked him about his first year as an undergraduate. "I got in touch with about half of these speakers after their talk. Of that group, I probably still keep in touch with one or two from each semester. . . . For example, James Fallows [national correspondent for *The Atlantic*] spoke here, and I was able to spend time with him, and now we e-mail and I hope to meet him again in the near future."

Beyond going to hear interesting speakers, Ben also makes a point of attending conferences on topics from entrepreneurship to politics to technology. His strategy is to identify venues with high ticket prices—"If the ticket price is too low, the people probably won't be quality"—and then try to convince the organizers to let him in free (or cheap) because of his student status. They're often surprisingly happy to help a bright, curious young person.

Ben's goal with these conferences is exposure to interesting things. He meets interesting people, he follows up, and this often leads him somewhere else interesting and unexpected.

"I was at a retreat in New Orleans held for ninety people in business, politics, journalism, and technology," Ben told me. "At dinner one night I was sitting next to a guy pretty high up in Democratic politics. He happened to be from Los Angeles. [Ben is also from California.] We stayed in touch over the next year, and then, about a month ago, he invited me to a dinner party. At the dinner were a congresswoman, state senators, movie studio execs, and various other high rollers. It was fascinating."

Ben doesn't know in advance exactly where these random encounters might lead, but he's discovered that it's usually somewhere interesting. I recommend that you adopt this same strategy. Focus on talks and conferences. If you're near a college campus, then monitor the speakers who visit. Such talks are usually open to the public, so you can attend. Also keep an eye on bookstores in your area, as they're a good place to find interesting speakers. Before you attend one of these talks, do some quick research on the person or field, and then think up an interesting question. After the talk, introduce yourself to the speaker and ask the question. There's great novelty in a high school student being engaged with big ideas, so the author is likely to remember you. Within a week or two, follow up with an e-mail.

The same basic approach can be used for conferences. Keep track of which events are coming through your nearest big city or college campus. Forget about buying tickets. Instead, contact the conference organizers directly and explain that you're a high school student and that you have a real interest in the topic. Ask about getting a "discounted" student pass—which, hopefully, they'll translate as "free." If you blog or write for your school newspaper, mention that you will write about your experience, thereby bringing the conference to the attention of a larger young audience. Another tactic is to get a teacher to agree to let you write a paper about the experience for extra credit or in place of another assignment. Conference organizers are susceptible to the argument that you're an eager young person trying to learn.

These tactics should get you started. In general, however, the more interesting people you meet, and the more conferences you attend, the more unique opportunities will arise. These opportunities, in turn, will build your interestingness to epic levels.

Pulling It All Together

This playbook is by far the largest of the three in this book, and for good reason: it provides the foundation for all of the other ideas and advice offered. Until you have free time in your schedule, and use that time to aggressively expose yourself to interesting things, you won't develop the deep interests needed to apply the advice in the parts of the book that follow. So take this advice seriously. It's among the most important that you'll encounter in these pages.

I want to conclude our discussion by summarizing the big-picture concepts that you've just learned. When you began Part 1, you were probably overworked—often scrambling to keep up with the haphazard mix of activities and hard classes that you hoped would impress the admissions staff at your dream school. Perhaps you found yourself frequently staying up late into the night to catch up on schoolwork, or losing whole afternoons and weekends to heavy extracurricular commitments.

Then I offered a radical alternative: *the ideal student workweek*. The idea is that during the average week you should be done with schoolwork by dinnertime on weekdays, and should work no more than one half day during the weekend.

We began your journey toward this goal with a focus on *streamlining*. You learned how to shave hours from your homework by taking better notes and rejecting rote review. You learned why paper writing should be spread over three days and why experimenting with your study habits is valuable. You heard my claim that Facebook is the tool of the devil—at least when it comes to procrastination—and learned about the power of environment and timing to get work done fast. You were then exposed to a dead-simple time management system that could eliminate schedule pileups and perhaps even defuse procrastination altogether.

For many students, this streamlining might be enough to get them down to the ideal student workweek. For some, however, even though these strategies will reduce their schedule footprint, their work demands still exceed the ideal. With this in mind, I next taught you the art of quitting, including how to take advantage of *the Final-Straw Effect* to defang your course load, and how to use the *Activity Andy test* to filter out activities that eat up time without earning you the respect of admissions officers.

With these strategies in place, you'll hopefully achieve the goal of injecting significant amounts of free time into your schedule. But what should you do with all of these newly liberated hours? This is where the second section of the playbook enters the scene with its advice for aggressive exploration. In it you learned the incredible power of developing a reading habit, and how to use communities to accelerate your path from a passing interest to something deep. You then learned about *the advice-guide method*, which provides step-by-step guidance for how to "crack the code" for a field of interest, jump-starting impressive work. And finally you heard about the power of meeting lots of interesting people and going to lots of interesting places.

All of this playbook advice serves the single simple idea motivating the law of underscheduling: If you want to be an admissions superstar, you need to have a deep interest, and the best way to develop such an interest is to inject large amounts of free time into your schedule and then use this time to aggressively explore things that catch your attention. The playbook spells out exactly how to make this idea a reality. All that's left is for you to get started.

Part 2

The Law of Focus

Master one serious interest. Don't waste time on unrelated activities.

The law of focus asks you to restrict your attention to a single serious extracurricular interest, and then work on this interest consistently over time until you become very good. Many students, however, fear that being good at only one thing is not enough to impress a jaded admissions staff. This law rejects that idea. It argues, instead, that when you focus intensely on a single interest you'll eventually reap significantly more rewards than if you had spread the same time among many things. In other words, being *the best* at one thing gets you further than being *good* at multiple things.

Relaxed superstars recognize this reality and use it to their advantage. It's much less stressful to keep your attention fixed on one pursuit than to juggle several. Such focus also happens to be a recipe for a richer, more fulfilling life. There's real pleasure to be gained from long-term mastery. Arguably, their dedication to the art of focus explains a lot about the Zen-like contentment most relaxed superstars seem to exude. This can all be yours as well—less stress, more impressiveness, access to the deepest secrets of happiness—if you're willing to let go of your instinct for doing more things and embrace the power of doing fewer things, and doing them better.

In Chapter 6, you'll hear the story of Michael, who is the personification of focus. He dedicated 100 percent of his extracurricular attention to a series of projects—each started only after the previous one had been completed—all dedicated to the topic of environmental sustainability. He was accepted at Stanford. Michael's story will help us structure our exploration of the law of focus. In subsequent chapters you'll learn how three scientific theories—the *Superstar Effect*, the *Matthew Effect*, and *countersignaling*—help explain why narrow attention yields such broad results. These theories argue, respectively, that you get an impressiveness bonus for being the best in a pursuit; that a high level of accomplishment in a single area generates extra accomplishments for little additional effort; and that in many cases doing more things can come across as less impressive. To emphasize these ideas, I'll tell you about a collection of other relaxed superstars who leveraged these effects to stand out during the admissions process. I'll conclude with a playbook that walks you through practical advice for getting started and then maintaining a focused lifestyle.

6

Solar Panels, Stress, and Stanford

IN JANUARY 2009, the one and a half million readers of the *Arizona Republic* encountered a photo of an increasingly familiar scene for this sun-soaked region: solar panels being installed on a roof. What made this photo stand out, however, was the accompanying article, and more specifically its surprisingly young subject. "Michael Silverman," it starts, "a senior at Phoenix County Day School, has a habit of turning golf carts into green machines." It details how this seventeen-year-old spearheaded the project to install these panels on his school's maintenance shed, where they'll provide renewable power to the school's fleet of golf carts.

Fast-forward a few months to the ribbon-cutting ceremony for the solar charging station. At the event, Michael, along with the school's principal, a group of proud teachers, and the mayor of Paradise Valley, stood on a platform facing a crowd of more than a hundred people. Behind the platform was the low-slung maintenance building—its rooftop air-conditioning condenser now flanked by rows of solar panels. Sunlight sparkled on their surface. After the ribbon was cut, the speeches began. Not long into the program, a teacher took the podium to say a few words about the project and its young manager. With a smile, he announced to the crowd: "When I grow up, I want to be just like Michael Silverman."

The effort behind this project began a year earlier, when Michael obtained a $5,000 grant from a local energy company. The school ended up approving an additional $40,000 to see the project to completion. This was Michael's second encounter with greening golf carts. During his sophomore year he had won a grant from the same energy company to convert a gas-powered golf cart to run on discarded cooking oil. A local entrepreneur later paid to ship the cart, along with Michael, to California to participate in a green technology exhibition. Everyone who knows Michael would admit that he developed an impressive skill for these sustainability projects. Later in the *Arizona Republic* article, for example, a teacher from Michael's school effuses: "[He's] got a great future ahead of him." Not surprising, the admissions officers at Michael's top-choice schools agreed.

Michael achieved some impressive feats. There's no doubt about that. Of equal importance, his feats were honored by the media. As he modestly admits: "I think third-party recognition of your efforts goes a really long way in admissions." But what makes him interesting for our study of relaxed superstars is that his work on green projects was his only extracurricular commitment. He didn't join multiple student groups. He wasn't a class officer. He didn't become secretary of the French club or compete in science fairs. Instead, his extracurricular schedule reads like a study in disciplined focus. In his sophomore year he won the grant to convert a golf cart to run on biodiesel. In his junior year he won the grant to install the solar panels. In his senior year he completed the solar panel installation in the fall, and then in the spring organized his school's Earth Day celebration.

That's it. He never had more than one activity at a time, and each new activity was focused on the same topic, environmental sustainability. Over time he got better and better at these projects, until he had teachers saying, only half-jokingly, that they wanted to be more like him.

Due to his streamlined schedule, Michael avoided the standard admissions-related stress that plagued his classmates. "It was a great lifestyle: I loved what I was doing," he told me. Michael was an aberration at the competitive private school he attended. The other students gunning for spots at schools like Stanford adopted a much more demanding strategy. "At my school, the thought was that you needed a 4.0 GPA," Michael notes. "In addition, you needed the usual activities: become a leader in student government and president of the senior class, join SADD [Students Against Drunk Driving], play varsity sports— that whole deal." Near-perfect SAT scores and a competitive course load were also expected.

Michael ignored this wisdom. In addition to keeping his activity load light he managed to keep his academic demands reasonable. During the notoriously difficult junior year, for example, when most of his classmates were taking four or five AP courses simultaneously, Michael took only one. When his classmates were pulling all-nighters to guarantee an A in every class, Michael was happy with the 3.6 GPA he earned by doing a reasonable amount of smart studying. As he explained: "If I knew I would get a B+ instead of an A− because I shifted my time around to work more on one of my sustainability projects, I was happy to do that." The same philosophy held for his SAT. "Standardized testing is not my strong point," he admitted. "I took the tests, did well enough, and kept most of my attention on my independent projects."

Reflecting on his numbers, Michael describes himself as having "a high enough GPA and scores to cross that threshold below which schools like Stanford automatically throw out your application—but not too much higher." He knew that if he could get to the holistic piece of the admissions process, where his essays, press clippings, and recommendations could be read, he would be competitive.

Another indicator of Michael's relaxed lifestyle was that during his time at Phoenix County Day School, four days out of five he would leave school after the final bell and hike to the summit of nearby Camelback Mountain. The hike would take at least an hour, sometimes twice as long. But as Michael explained: "No matter what work I had, it didn't matter, I went hiking—to help me relax, chill out, and figure out the smartest way to handle what I had to do."

Michael wasn't lazy. He wasn't avoiding work for the sake of avoiding work. He was taking a calculated risk. He decided to focus his attention on a small number of projects all related to the same subject. (On his Web site, he goes so far as to give himself a tagline: "The Sustainability Student.") If he had adopted a harder course schedule, or joined a dozen other clubs, he would have lost the ability to make such amazing progress on his single point of focus. "It just wouldn't have been feasible," he told me. "That's the bottom line." And without that focused progress, he would have been another overcommitted kid, failing to stand out.

Michael's risk paid off. He was able to enjoy his high school career *and* get accepted to Stanford, his dream school. The rest of Part 2 explores the focus strategy adopted by students like Michael. In the chapters that follow, you'll learn exactly why keeping your attention fixed on one thing can prove so effective—even though it requires less work and stress than the standard approaches to becoming a star. By the time you've moved on to the practical advice of the playbook, I'll hopefully have converted you to this philosophy of focused effort.

7

The Superstar Effect

THE HIGHLIGHT of the 2008 season of the Metropolitan Opera in New York was its production of Gaetano Donizetti's *La Fille du Régiment*. Among professional opera singers, Donizetti's work is known as the Mount Everest of opera. This reputation is due, almost entirely, to an especially devilish aria, "Ah! Mes amis, quel jour de fête," written for the tenor role of Tonis. The aria arrives early in the performance, before the singer has time to fully warm his vocal cords, and makes a near-impossible demand: hitting nine high Cs in a row, the final note held in a long, punishing sustain. The difficulty of this feat cannot be overestimated. "The alluring note has made and ended operatic careers," noted a critic for the *New York Times*, "and [has] even helped drive one star to suicide." Not surprisingly, most tenors, when faced with this Mount Everest aria, default to the far easier natural C.

It was for all of these reasons that when tenor Juan Diego Flórez nailed the high C nine times in a row during his 2008 performance at the Met, the feat made international news. The acclaim for Flórez's performance was so intense that the Met reversed its informal ban on encores, allowing Flórez to feed the crowd's desire for more. The audience kept clapping until he sang the aria one more time.

Opera singers, among their other eccentricities, are notoriously private about money. We can estimate from indirect sources, however, that a top singer at a top venue, such as the Met, likely makes in the tens of thousands of dollars per performance. This income is supplemented by CD sales. While few classical CDs become true blockbusters, winning an industry award can ensure a healthy flow of royalty payments. A talent like Flórez, therefore, likely makes a very comfortable, though probably not lavish, living as a professional singer.

But then there are the superstars. In 1972, thirty-six years before Florez's acclaimed performance, a young tenor by the name of Luciano Pavarotti sang the role of Tonis in *La Fille du Régiment*. The power of Pavarotti's high Cs in this performance was stunning. Terry Teachout, drama critic for the *Wall Street Journal*, has called them "sunlit." The audience at the Met demanded a record seventeen curtain calls—making Florez's acclaim seem mild by comparison. Soon after the performance, opera buffs began to call Pavarotti the King of the High Cs. He became a superstar performer, selling out stadiums and earning a worldwide following.

Pavarotti's voice was better than Flórez's. Writing about Flórez's 2008 performance of *La Fille*, for example, the *New York Times* critic noted: "If truth be told, it's not as hard as it sounds for a tenor with a light lyric voice like Mr. Flórez to toss off those high Cs. . . . [In] the early 1970's, when Luciano Pavarotti . . . let those high Cs ring out, that was truly astonishing." But this advantage of Pavarotti over Flórez could be considered slight, since few singers can hit those notes at all. If we had to rank the talent of opera tenors, we might place Pavarotti at the very top, but Juan Diego Flórez not far below.

Minor differences in talent, however, can generate major differences in rewards. We speculated earlier that Flórez receives a good, but not a lavish, income. By contrast, when Pavarotti died in 2007, sources estimated his estate was worth $275–$475 *million*. His advantage in vocal ability made the difference between a nice career and a fortune.

This story has surprising implications for our quest to understand the college admissions process. As I'll argue below, the same effect that explains the gap between Pavarotti's and Flórez's fortunes can explain why relaxed superstars receive so many more admissions rewards than their hardworking student peers.

The Superstar Effect

It was this Superstar Effect—the idea that the most talented in a field earn disproportionately more rewards than those who are only slightly less talented—that piqued the curiosity of an economist named Sherwin Rosen. He was intrigued by the question of why the best opera singers, movie stars, authors, and actors, among other talents, make so much more money than peers who are only slightly less skilled. In a paper titled "The Economics of Superstars," published in the *American Economic Review* in 1981, Rosen worked through the mathematics of why the best so soundly outearn their closest rivals.

The details of Rosen's equations are hard for a nonspecialist to follow, but the basic ideas they capture are intuitive. Let's return to our example of Pavarotti and Flórez. As we established, both are regarded as phenomenal tenors—better than all but perhaps a few singers in the world—but Pavarotti's sunlit voice had a slight edge over Flórez's. Now imagine a million opera fans logging onto iTunes to buy an opera album. These fans, being savvy, may have heard that Pavarotti is *slightly* better than Flórez. Perhaps they read that same *New York Times* piece, pining for the power of a young Pavarotti. These fans are more likely, therefore, to buy Pavarotti's album—if you have just $10 to spend, why not buy the very best? The effect of a million listeners each making this rational decision about which album to buy ends up assigning most of the $10 million they collectively spend to Pavarotti. In other words, he earns disproportionately more money than Flórez, even though the difference in talent may be slight. This same argument can apply to a variety of talents, from blockbuster movie stars to bestselling authors. They all share the same underlying narrative of the very best earning a huge share of the rewards in their field.

College admissions, I argue, is one of the settings where the Superstar Effect plays an important role. As I explain below, relaxed superstars take advantage of this reality by focusing their energy on becoming a Pavarotti in a single pursuit, instead of burning out by trying to become a Flórez in many different pursuits.

The Academic Superstar

There are two areas in which the Superstar Effect can play an important role in college admissions. The first is academic performance. Rosen's theory predicts that a valedictorian would receive a disproportionate amount of rewards compared to students who are very near the top of the class, but not number one. A researcher named Paul Atwell put this idea to the test in a 2001 paper published in the journal *Sociology of Education*. Atwell studied a collection of elite public and private high schools. These schools were among the most demanding in the country. To put this in perspective, in 1997, when Atwell began the study, only about 0.7 percent of test-takers nationwide scored 780 or higher on the verbal section of the SAT. In fact, over 80 percent of high schools in the country had *no* students who scored this high, while an additional 12 percent had only a single student who crossed this mark. The elite schools studied by Atwell, by contrast, had on average at least ten such high scorers.

Atwell entered these bastions of talent to look for the Superstar Effect. His main research tool was the AI (Academic Index) formula used by Dartmouth College's admissions staff to rank each applicant's academic performance with a single score from 1 to 9. The formula combines SAT I and SAT II scores along with a value known as the converted class rank, which is an adjusted version of class rank that attempts to equalize differences between schools of different calibers. The appeal of the Dartmouth scale is that there exist good data connecting AI scores to acceptance probabilities. Atwell used the data to explore how students at the very top of their class at top high schools would fare as compared to those only slightly below. (He focused on top high schools because they tend to have large clusters of students near the top of the class with similar academic performance. Less-competitive schools are more likely to have a small number of outliers outpace the rest of their class by a considerable distance.)

As Atwell reports in his paper, his results matched the predictions of the Superstar Effect. He discovered that being number one in your class provides an increase in acceptance probabilities that's equivalent to adding an extra 70 points to your SAT I scores and 60 points to your SAT II scores. To better understand this result, consider the case of two exceptional students, whom I'll call Peter and Tina. They both have 770 math and verbal scores on the SAT I (Atwell's research was conducted before the introduction of the writing section) and an average score of 760 on their SAT II tests. Assume their extracurricular activities are comparable. Here's where things get interesting: Peter is number one in his class while Tina is number ten in hers. From the perspective of their grade point averages, these two ranks are essentially identical. At a school of the caliber of those studied by Atwell, the difference between the number one and number ten ranked student likely reduces to a couple of tenths, if not hundredths, of a GPA point—a difference that can be generated by a few A-minuses instead of As over four years of school. Logically speaking, Peter's and Tina's admissions chances at Dartmouth should be near identical. How much can a few tenths of a decimal point on a GPA really help Peter? The data studied by Atwell, however, reveal that the Superstar Effect ensures that these extra points do matter—*a lot*. Peter, as it turns out, has a 94 percent chance of being accepted at Dartmouth while Tina has only a 74 percent chance. In other words, the Superstar Effect gave Peter a 20 percent boost in admissions chances even though he was clearly nowhere near 20 percent more talented than Tina.

If we make Peter and Tina slightly less competitive, the effect becomes even more dramatic. For the sake of example, reduce their SAT I scores slightly, to 750 on each section, and their SAT II scores to 740 on average. Assume Peter is still valedictorian but Tina is now ranked number five in her class. The same 20 percent gap in admissions chances remains, even though the difference in their academic records is vanishingly small. If you drop the scores down to around 700, Peter the valedictorian remains in the running for Dartmouth with a 75 percent admission probability while Tina, still yapping at Peter's heels in the number five spot, has only a 25 percent chance of admission!

The conclusion is unavoidable. When it comes to grades, the Superstar Effect plays an enormous role. Being the number one student in your class provides a significant boost in your admissions chances as compared to those students with slightly lower GPAs. In this study, Peter was Pavarotti and Tina was Flórez. The slight difference in academic ability between the two students generated significant differences in their admissions fortunes.

But there's a problem here. Attempting to become valedictorian is an *incredibly* risky strategy. The Superstar Effect is a double-edged sword. It pours lavish rewards on those who become the best in their field, but it remains savagely indifferent to those who fall just short. It's very difficult to become valedictorian. It's also very stressful. You have to obsess over every test for your full high school career, and just one or two poor performances can scuttle your mission to become the best. And as we learned from Atwell's research, even if you *barely* fall short of the top spot—for example ending up number five instead of number one in class rank—you lose the admissions bonus enjoyed by the valedictorian. One bad midterm can render four years of stress and anxiety worthless.

I described Atwell's research because it proves that college admissions is not immune from the Superstar Effect. But attempting to generate the effect using your class rank clearly violates the spirit of the relaxed superstar philosophy. With this in mind, I ask that you take your newfound respect for the effect and apply it to the second area of admissions where your performance plays a big role: extracurricular activities. It is here that generating the Superstar Effect is much easier and much less risky than attempting to juice your GPA.

The Extracurricular Superstar

Imagine that you're an admissions officer reading through a pile of applications when you come across a particularly strong student. The student—let's call him Alex—has good grades and test scores, and he devoted a lot of effort to become the editor of the school newspaper, president of the student body, and an officer in the model UN club. The problem for Alex is that you, the admissions officer, have probably already reviewed applications from students who have done just as well as he in these activities, if not better. Maybe you saw a budding reporter who published articles in a local newspaper, a student body president who helped initiate major changes at his school, and an international relations wonk who won awards at national model UN conferences. Alex, therefore, is not the *best* you've seen this year in any of his major pursuits—he may have reached Flórez caliber in these activities, but he fell short of Pavarotti-style brilliance. This doesn't mean that you'll automatically reach for the "reject" stamp, but there's no Superstar Effect at play to help Alex get a disproportionate share of your attention.

Now imagine that you come across the application for a student named Jennifer. The application emphasizes one extracurricular pursuit: an obsession with learning about Geminid meteors. As a young child, she saw an exhibit on meteors that snagged her attention and refused to let go. By the time she applied to college, she had become a minor expert who was known by many of the scientists in the field. Presumably you would be more captivated by Jennifer than by Alex. It's unlikely that any other student you've seen this year was better on the subject of space objects. She was the best in her field, and thus the Superstar Effect works its magic.

As it turns out, this is exactly what happened. Jennifer, who is a real student, was accepted into MIT. The same year that she applied, I happened to have a meeting with one of MIT's admissions officers to talk about their selection process. He mentioned Jennifer as one of their favorite applicants for her class. He described her as "a world expert on meteors." In his mind, her status as the best in her field helped her stand out as an applicant. It's hard to turn down a world expert.

I didn't get a chance to meet the real Jennifer, but I've met students like her. If I had to guess, I would say that the time required for her to pursue her obsession in meteors was *significantly* less than the time required to maintain three major structured activities as Alex, our hypothetical student, did. Therefore, even though Jennifer invested fewer total hours than hardworking Alex, the Superstar Effect put her ahead in the admissions process.

This phenomenon is so important that I've extracted it into its own hypothesis:

> **The Extracurricular Superstar Hypothesis, Part 1**
> You will receive a sizable impressiveness bonus for an extracurricular pursuit if you're the best at that pursuit out of all of the applicants the admissions officers have encountered that year.

We see this hypothesis verified in the obvious examples of applicants who played violin at Carnegie Hall or competed in the Olympics. Their uncontested talent makes them incredibly desirable to admissions officers. But our example of Jennifer demonstrates an important nuance: she was the best space-rock expert MIT had seen, but then again, there aren't that many student-aged space-rock experts. We can imagine, therefore, that her accomplishment was far easier than those boasted by the Carnegie Hall performer and the Olympic athlete—in their fields there is *lots* of competition.

This observation leads to a natural follow-up hypothesis:

> **The Extracurricular Superstar Hypothesis, Part 2**
> The Superstar Effect bonus holds regardless of the competitiveness of the activity for which you are the best. Therefore, pursuits that do not have lots of competition yield a higher ratio of impressiveness to hours of work required than those that do.

Put another way, becoming a meteor expert is much easier than becoming one of the nation's best young violinists. The impressiveness bonus, however, will be similar for both.

Before concluding this chapter, I have to address an important caveat. Some students interpret the Extracurricular Superstar Hypothesis as a pitch to do something *unusual*. "If I'm the only applicant who took underwater banjo lessons," they think, "then by default I'm the best at this pursuit and will get the Superstar Effect bonus." Alas, things aren't quite so simple. This final hypothesis adds an important qualification to the above ideas:

> **The Extracurricular Superstar Hypothesis, Part 3**
> In order to qualify you as "the best" in an extracurricular pursuit, your efforts must demonstrate *some* marker of exceptional ability. It's not enough that the pursuit is unusual; you must also appear to be unusually good.

Consider the following example of this hypothesis playing out in the real world. An infamously snide article titled "The Swarm of College Super-Applicants," published in *New York Magazine* in 2006, included a profile of a student named Vadim from Brooklyn Technical High School. Vadim was involved in many standard activities, but his most distinctive extracurricular was Ping-Pong. He started a club at his school and even took some outside lessons. This is certainly an unusual pursuit. At the schools where he applied—which included Yale, Cornell, and Columbia—he was probably the only student to list this activity on his application that year. But this uniqueness is not enough to generate the Superstar Effect. Starting a club and taking a few lessons do not qualify as a "marker of exceptional ability," as required by the third part of our Extracurricular Superstar Hypothesis. Therefore, this activity remains simply unusual—not unusually impressive.

The admissions expert hired by *New York Magazine* to critique the superapplicants agreed with this assessment. "Yale, Cornell, and Columbia might be a stretch," she said. She went on to call the Ping-Pong club a "red flag," potentially indicating that he's a "serial joiner."

If Vadim had gone further with this activity, perhaps getting to competition level, or using his skills as an excuse to travel to China and connect with student-aged players of the sport, then the effect would be different. A "red flag" activity might, in this case, be transformed into an indication of a superstar. Once the admissions officers started thinking about Vadim as "the world-class Ping-Pong player," he would become hard to forget. But without some marker of exceptional ability, Ping-Pong remains yet another random activity.

If you recall Michael Silverman, the student profiled in the previous chapter, you'll see a good example of all three parts of the Extracurricular Superstar Hypothesis working together. Michael didn't outwork his classmates. As I established, their quest for 4.0 GPAs and long activity lists required more total hours than Michael spent on his singular focus on environmental sustainability. But by the time his application crossed the desk of a Stanford admissions officer, he was most likely the best "green" student they had seen that year. You can imagine the admissions officers, taking their cue from the slogan on his Web site, starting to call him "the sustainability student," as in, "I really think the sustainability student would make a great addition to our incoming class." In this way he satisfied the first two parts of the hypothesis. He satisfied the third part, the requirement for markers of exceptional ability in the pursuit, by including press clippings about his feats with his application. Third-party recognition provides powerful validation that you did something that required ability.

If you become the best at a single pursuit out of all the

applicants applying to the same school that year, and then demonstrate this required real ability, you'll enjoy the avalanche of bonus impressiveness predicted by the Extracurricular Superstar Hypothesis. And as in the examples of Jennifer and Michael, conquering one activity can actually be much easier than doing very well in many. This is the magic of the Superstar Effect: doing less can make you more impressive. That is why the Superstar Effect is a powerful weapon in the relaxed superstar arsenal.

8

Good Begets Good

IN LATE spring 2008, Our Lady of Consolation, a Catholic church in Wayne, New Jersey, was filled to capacity. Almost two hundred seniors from nearby De Paul Catholic High School, along with their proud families, had gathered for the traditional baccalaureate mass, held the night before the De Paul graduation ceremony. As the service ended, Sister Jeanne, a respected nun and the vice principal of academics at De Paul, took the pulpit to begin the award ceremony that follows the mass. Most of the awards were certificates of excellence, given to individual students who had done especially well in specific classes. These winners had been notified earlier in the week and therefore were waiting with nervous anticipation for their name to be called.

One student among the crowd, however, felt no nervousness. His name was Kevin. Though he was a good student, he hadn't received any phone calls about winning a certificate, so he didn't worry about being summoned into the spotlight that evening.

But then Sister Jeanne moved on to the Delta Award. This was to be given to the single student who over the past *four years* had shown the most excellence in mathematics. The winner wasn't necessarily the student with the best grades, but was instead chosen at the teachers' discretion for having been particularly engaged in the classroom.

Sister Jeanne announced the winner.

Kevin was startled. "Did she just say my name?" he wondered. He scanned the crowded church to see if his friends had turned in his direction, to make sure he had heard correctly before he stood up to claim his unexpected prize.

Five minutes later, the scene repeated. Sister Jeanne announced the Thomas Jefferson Award for excellence over four years in history and social studies. Once again, Kevin was surprised to hear his name called as the winner. Then, at the culmination of the event, when the award for the most outstanding male student of the graduating class was announced, Kevin won yet again. The quiet night he'd expected had been replaced by a flurry of major awards that made him the obvious star of the De Paul Catholic High School class of 2008.

Kevin's story interests me because he defies our expectations for the type of student who wins stacks of awards. We assume that it's the brilliant valedictorian who runs a dozen different clubs who is named the most outstanding math, history, social studies, and general overall student of his graduating class. Kevin, however, doesn't match this description. Consider, for example, his experience in math class. As he explained: "My teachers didn't love me because I was the smartest kid; we had whiz kids in my math classes, and I wasn't one of them." Or consider his light extracurricular schedule. Baseball and Boy Scouts were his only significant extracurricular obligations throughout his high school career. He eventually made the varsity baseball squad and reached the Eagle Scout rank. "Wait," you may be thinking, "playing one sport might not be too bad, but becoming an Eagle Scout is a time-intensive activity!" While this is true over the long term (the process starts at the age of twelve), its short-term demands are reasonable. As Kevin explained to me, a lot of the work on his merit badges, for example, was confined to annual summer camp, and he estimates that during the school year he committed around two to three hours per week to scouting—hardly a schedule-devouring endeavor.

As you might imagine, this light extracurricular load supported a relaxed lifestyle. "I was watching my friends stressing themselves trying to keep up with eight different activities," he told me. "But because my schedule wasn't bogged down, I could take that spontaneous trip to the shore, or into the city, or just enjoy myself." Not only did Kevin's focus generate relaxation, but it also provided him tangible rewards in the college admissions process. With his slew of awards, and the stellar recommendations that come with being crowned your school's favorite student (the school's chaplain, for example, wrote him a powerful letter), Kevin easily earned a place at his reach school, Georgetown University.

How did Kevin win these awards and recognition, and then ultimately get accepted at Georgetown, without being a whiz kid or overcommitted? In this chapter, I argue that his success can be ascribed to a curious phenomenon dubbed the *Matthew Effect*. To understand this effect, and the rewards it generates, I will take you on a brief journey that extends from academia practices in nineteenth-century France to the patterns of citations in scientific journals, and then onward to modern college admissions.

The Forty-first Chair

It's frustrating to attend school with a student like Kevin. It's not that he did anything wrong or underhanded, it's just that everything seemed to go his way. In calculus class, when the teacher asked the students to split up into groups to work on problems, Kevin's classmates gravitated to him with their questions. He wasn't the best student in the class, but he was the most patient, and he had a knack for working through concepts with others. After a while his teacher started to quip, "If you have a problem, ask Kevin; if Kevin doesn't know, then you can ask me." It's not surprising, therefore, that he won the Delta Award for most outstanding math student—even though he wasn't the smartest or highest scoring. The teachers loved him.

He won the matching award in history and social studies under similar circumstances, even though, once again, other students were academically stronger in the subjects. Along the same lines, he was made the captain of the baseball team, even though he wasn't the best player, and was named the most outstanding male graduate, even though other students had better grades and more demanding extracurriculars. It's not that Kevin didn't deserve his awards and recognition; it's just that other students did as well. Accolades were attracted to Kevin, as if pulled by a magnetic force.

A nineteenth-century French novelist named Arsène Houssaye would understand the frustration of Kevin's peers. In 1855 he coined the phrase "the forty-first chair" to describe the plight of talented individuals, deserving of rewards, who are nevertheless bypassed as these rewards are garnered by a select few. Houssaye's phrase was inspired by the French Academy—l'Académie française. This elite institution, founded in 1635 by the chief minister to Louis XIII, survives to this day as the official protector of the French language (and the unofficial molten core of French snobbery). Some of its most recent activities include the declaration that *courriel* is now the official French word for "e-mail" (even though French speakers had been happily using the English word for years), and that a blog should be referred to as *un blogue*.

L'Académie has only forty seats. If you're elected to a seat you retain the position for life. These positions are so important to French society that the members of l'Académie are called "the immortals." An immortal, upon first taking his (or, in an unfortunately small number of cases, *her*) seat, must begin by eulogizing the deceased member he replaces. The new member is then issued *l'habit vert*, the official uniform for formal ceremonies. Last updated in the era of Napoleon, the outfit includes a sweeping black robe with wide lapels embroidered with green leaves. It's topped by an eighteenth-century-style two-cornered hat adorned with black feathers. The men get swords. It's all wonderfully French, which is to say ridiculously ceremonial and uptight.

The 710 immortals who have held seats in the academy since the early nineteenth century include some of France's most famous citizens, from Dumas to Poincairé to Voltaire. But when Houssaye coined the term "the forty-first chair" in 1855, he was referencing the equally impressive list of talented French writers and thinkers who *never* gained a seat—a list that includes Descartes, Proust, and Verne. Their exclusion from l'Académie was not due to lack of ability. It was just that space was limited, and you had to have perfect timing and connections to enter the ranks of the immortals.

Jump forward a century to 1968. It was then that the sociologist Robert K. Merton referenced Houssaye's forty-first chair in his paper "The Matthew Effect in Science," which he published, appropriately enough, in the prestigious journal *Science*. Merton noted that the phenomenon of the forty-first chair was alive and well in the world of modern scientific research. He pointed to the winners of the Nobel Prize in various sciences. "[It is] a well-known fact," wrote Merton, "that a good number of scientists who have not received the prize and will not receive it have contributed as much as some of the recipients, or more." His explanation centered on fame. Better-known scientists get more recognition than their lesser-known colleagues, which makes them even more well-known, and gets them even more recognition, and so on. He noted, for example, that if two scientists publish a similar result at the same time, the more famous scientist will almost always get credit, and if multiple scientists coauthor a paper, the most famous of the coauthors is the most likely to be associated with the finding.

Merton called this phenomenon the Matthew Effect, in reference to a verse from the Gospel of Matthew: "For unto every one that hath, more shall be given, and he shall have abundance: but from him that hath not shall be taken away even that which he hath." Put plainly, the rich get richer while the poor get poorer. In the sciences, this means that once you get some fame you will reap more rewards and therefore become more famous and then get more rewards, in a self-reinforcing loop, while your less-famous colleagues are relegated to the forty-first chair.

Since Merton first identified this effect, the notion has been applied in a variety of contexts. In his 2008 book *Outliers*, for example, Malcolm Gladwell highlighted a surprising example of the effect in action. He noted that in the Canadian Junior Hockey League, players who were born in the early months of the year are more likely to make it to the pros. As Gladwell explains, when a kid first joins the league, he's assigned to a team based on his birth year. Where exactly he's born in that year, Gladwell argues, can make a big difference in eventual ability. If a player was born in January 1985, for example, then when he joins a team with a 1985 cutoff he's almost a year older than his teammates born in December of the same year. At this early stage, a difference of almost a year in age translates into big differences in size and ability. These larger and stronger young hockey players, born in the early months of the year, are more likely to be tracked into youth all-star teams and receive extra coaching. This increases their advantage over their slightly younger peers, leading to more special attention and even faster growth of their abilities. Over the years, the extra coaching and confidence accumulate to provide these players a significant edge over their later-born teammates. A small early advantage grows into something large.

Now that you understand the effect, I'll show you how it plays a major role in the subject of most interest to us: college admissions. To begin, I'll turn our focus back to the story of our friend Kevin the Eagle Scout, and his unlikely rise to become his school's favorite student.

Kevin's Abundance

To understand Kevin's success, consider his main focus: becoming an Eagle Scout. When you think about scouting, you probably conjure images of pocketknives and knot tying. But as any committed Boy Scout will tell you, the real goal of the program is to teach the subtle art of leadership.

"I was a patrol leader at age twelve," Kevin told me. "I would have to go into the woods and be responsible for three, four, maybe five guys. You learn quickly how to relate to their issues, to figure out what they need, and how you can help them."

This leadership training intensified as Kevin moved up through the scouting ranks. By his junior year of high school, for example, when he launched the community service project required to reach Eagle Scout, Kevin was supervising a team of eleven younger scouts in a year-long effort to digitize the records of a local history museum.

Seen in this light, the path to Eagle Scout can be understood as a half-decade-long process of leadership training. At an age when most students still struggle to organize a group of friends to agree on plans for Friday night, Kevin had already spent years honing his ability to understand his peers and coordinate their efforts. He had an abundance of leadership talent, and as the Matthew Effect predicts, this early advantage began to attract and accumulate more and more advantages as he progressed through high school.

When Kevin was fifteen, for example, he joined the summer-league baseball team of a nearby town. By the second game of the season, Kevin's leadership ability was well established. "Most fifteen-year-olds wouldn't get a chance to get a word in edgewise with the coach, but he allowed it with me," Kevin recalls. He was named the team captain by unanimous consent, even though the team had several older players. When he made his high school's varsity baseball squad a couple of years later, his leadership virtuosity once again earned him the role of captain.

As another example, consider his success in math. Kevin wasn't the smartest student in his classes, but his leadership skills, honed by scouting, made him a focal point of his struggling classmates' questions. It was this that earned him his teachers' respect, and then, eventually, the award for the most outstanding math student.

The deeper you dig into Kevin's story, the more you see that such advantages accumulated in almost every aspect of his high school career. After Kevin's successes in the classroom and on the playing field, for example, he was a natural pick for his school's peer-ministry program, which requires a small group of seniors to work with the administration to help younger students. Once in this program, Kevin's skills made him a standout. "The chaplain gave me all of these leadership roles," he recalls. "Without my leadership experience, he wouldn't have come to me; there were lots of kids who had similar ideas, but they didn't know how to implement them." Kevin, by contrast, was a maestro of organizing young people to complete goals. (When you're faced with a setting sun, a pile of firewood, an uncooked dinner, and a group of hungry scouts, you quickly learn how to spur people into action.) "I knew how to change things on the fly, react to issues, and address problems as they arose," Kevin said. The chaplain, like many of the other teachers at De Paul Catholic High School, became a supporter of the young scout, eventually adding a glowing recommendation letter to the many that helped Kevin get into Georgetown.

When I confronted Kevin with the long list of leadership positions and awards he had accumulated throughout his high school career, he modestly sidestepped my praise.

"You have to understand," he pleaded, "I had been training to lead people since I was twelve."

Kevin's story is a pristine example of the Matthew Effect in action. His early involvement in the Boy Scouts gave him an edge over his peers in terms of leadership skills. This early advantage began to accumulate additional advantages: minor leadership roles that led to major leadership roles that led to awards and powerful recommendations—and then college acceptance. Eventually, Kevin became good enough at his one skill that he was vaulted into the ranks of his school's "immortals," while his talented, but not excellent, classmates remained stuck in the forty-first chair.

The Complementary-Accomplishments Hypothesis

As should be clear by now, the Matthew Effect provides strong support for the law of focus. If you're like Kevin, and you focus on becoming very good at a single pursuit (in his case, leadership), this initial abundance will attract more abundance. Over time, the rewards will accumulate faster and faster until you're catapulted into superstardom. The magic of the Matthew Effect is that once you've invested the time required to become good at a single thing, additional rewards come with little extra effort. By spending a reasonable amount of time on just one thing, you can end up with more impressive accomplishments, and less stress, than the student who spends a lot of time spread over many different things.

This idea is important enough to merit its own hypothesis:

> **The Complementary-Accomplishments Hypothesis**
> Once you accomplish something that is unambiguously impressive, you'll begin to achieve complementary accomplishments with little additional effort.

Imagine two students, Amy and Tom. They both want an impressive college application. Amy chooses three independent pursuits: volunteering at the local hospital, playing the flute in the band, and becoming a student council officer. Because time spent on any one of these activities doesn't help the others, she has to devote separate blocks of time to each. She decides to spend ten hours per week per activity. Over time, she becomes a senior volunteer at the hospital, second-chair flute in the band, and secretary of the student council. It's exhausting work, but she's serious about getting into college.

Now consider Tom. Unlike Amy, he decides to focus on a single pursuit: computer programming. He plans to dedicate fifteen hours per week to it. That's a lot of time for a single activity, but it's only half the total time Amy devoted to her extracurriculars.

Spending fifteen hours a week, Tom makes fast progress. He starts contributing to an open-source-programming project and builds his own iPhone application. This lands him a competitive summer internship with a technology company. The company then sponsors him to compete in the prestigious ACM student programming competition, where he places well. He's soon asked to join his school's Science Bowl team to handle the technology questions. At the same time, his skill helps him ace the computer science courses offered by his high school, and this qualifies him to continue his study of the subject at the local university. (Many schools have such arrangements with nearby colleges.)

By the time Tom graduates, his résumé seems longer, more interesting, and more impressive than Amy's, even though he spent only half the number of hours per week on extracurriculars. Amy became *good* at three things, but didn't become *great* at any. Therefore, she had to invest significant time to earn every accomplishment. Tom, by contrast, became unambiguously great at programming. Because he reached this high level, he was rewarded with an avalanche of complementary accomplishments that required little extra effort on his part. The end result was a better résumé that required less effort and stress.

Two Real Superstars

Amy and Tom were hypothetical characters whose stories I constructed to present the hypothesis in an easy-to-grasp manner. Their story, however, is more common for real students than you might imagine. For example, below I describe the accomplishments of two students chosen by USA *Today* for a list of the twenty most impressive high school seniors in the country. I think we can agree that they qualify as superstars. For each, I'll explain exactly where the Complementary-Accomplishments Hypothesis helped fuel their success.

Arnav
A four-time qualifier for the U.S.A. Mathematical Olympiad summer program; gold medal at the International Mathematical Olympiad in Ljubljana, Slovenia; U.S. Physics Team; winner of numerous math competitions, including the U.S.A. Mathematical Olympiad and the Mandelbrot Competition; math club; leader of state math team to American Regional Mathematics League championship; member of Science Bowl team that placed third nationally.

Arnav's accomplishments list can be overwhelming when you first encounter it. You see award after award, competition after competition, until, eventually, you declare that he must be a genius. I don't know Arnav, but I've spent a half decade at MIT, so I do know about students like him. When I read the above description I don't see an untouchable genius. Instead I see a student who focused on becoming very good at a very specific skill: competition math. This skill is a different beast from academic math. Raw quantitative intelligence is less important here than practicing solving certain types of math puzzles under tight time constraints. Arnav focused on this specific skill and eventually got very good at it. Everything else in his description is a complementary accomplishment attracted by this base skill. Once you're good at competition math, you'll be invited to participate on a variety of teams in a variety of competitions. Each of these participations, however, does not require a distinct application of effort; they all result from the original push to become good at this specific type of math.

In fact, I would wager that Arnav's schedule was probably less stressful than his résumé suggests. He no doubt devoted many hours to practicing competition math, and he traveled to competitions at least a few times a year, but such a schedule is still probably easier than trying to juggle a large collection of unrelated activities, each requiring its own serious weekly time commitment. The Complementary-Accomplishments Hypothesis allowed Arnav to transform an initial advantage into overwhelming abundance.

Here's another example:

> **Geoffrey**
> Researched mechanisms for fatigue and deformation in crystals, finding photon emissions may help predict material failures in crystals; named Siemens Competition regional finalist and Intel Science Talent Search semifinalist; won second- and third-place grand awards at the International Science & Engineering Fair; named school Science Bowl president and computing club president; mentor for middle school math team.

Don't let the technical phrases like "deformation in crystals" and "photon emissions" fool you into just assuming that Geoffrey is the next Einstein. You must soldier past the "wow" factor of these details to deconstruct the reality of Geoffrey's path. I looked up his research to get a better idea of what he accomplished. Put simply, his work involves hooking up a sensitive light sensor to a computer and then bending a piece of material near the sensor. Some basic physics reveals that when you bend certain materials they emit photons. The light sensor can detect these photons and therefore reveal information about the stresses being placed on the bent material.

The first point you should recognize is that Geoffrey did not come up with this idea by himself. The open secret of major science fairs is that participants are almost always coached by a scientist who helps them select an experiment and then guides them through the process. The judges of the fairs know this fact. They're happy to admit that they're not evaluating the ability of these students to generate original research insights. Instead, they're testing the students' ability to understand and discuss the science behind their coached experiments.

Learning the science, of course, is not easy. And the students still have to master the technology needed to make the experiments work. But this is a more tractable challenge than generating original scientific breakthroughs—which is what people assume is going on when they hear about high school students involved in research. I imagine Geoffrey focused on learning two specific things—some basic material physics and the basics of programming computers—as these are the skills needed to run his experiment. As with Arnav, almost everything in Geoffrey's list can be seen as a complementary accomplishment generated by his proficiency in these narrowly defined skills. The science fairs, the computing club, the Science Bowl, mentoring the junior high school math team—these are all opportunities made available because Geoffrey became good at physics and computers. These skills aren't trivial, but they're not prohibitively difficult or stressful to obtain either. The Complementary-Accomplishments Hypothesis explains what transformed a reasonable amount of focused effort into a stunning résumé.

Michael and Matthew

To conclude, I want to return to the story of Michael Silverman—the focused student described in the opening of Part 2. In the previous chapter, I argued that the Superstar Effect played an important role in Michael's admissions success. Here I'll argue that the Matthew Effect was at work as well.

Let's start by tracing the key steps in Michael's rise to prominence. During his freshman year of high school, Michael and a friend pitched an independent-project idea to their teachers. They proposed a somewhat ambiguous plan to design a house of the future. When discussing this idea, they learned from one of their teachers about a grant program run by a local energy company. The program was intended to fund student groups looking to build sustainable energy projects. The teacher who told them about the project helped them apply for the grant. To improve their chances, however, they abandoned their wishy-washy house design idea for something more concrete: converting a golf cart to run on biodiesel. After winning a $5,000 grant, they found a retired engineer who had the expertise to help them complete the conversion. He was also willing to volunteer unlimited time, which was fortunate, because Michael and his friend knew nothing about engineering. By the time this project was completed, Michael had honed a specific skill: raising money for sustainability projects and then seeing them through to completion. (Remember, he put all of his time into making this project work—avoiding any other extracurricular entanglements.)

From this initial ability multiple complementary accomplishments began to blossom. After finishing the golf cart conversion, Michael submitted a new grant to the energy company. His proposal was to add solar panels to the school's maintenance shed. With a solid track record behind him, he found that the company was quick to award him the second grant. This allowed Michael to start the project, but it soon began clear that more money was needed. At this point, however, he could demonstrate to his school's administration that he had received multiple grants and completed similar projects. This gave him enough credibility to get the additional funding needed to complete the work. Soon the press started to write articles about this environmental wunderkind. People at a nonprofit in California read these articles and invited Michael and his friend to come present their biodiesel golf cart at a major exhibit on alternative energy. By the time he applied to Stanford, Michael was a star.

Michael modestly describes his rise as a sequence of lucky

breaks. But we know better. Through our newly trained eyes, we see a core ability attracting complementary opportunities and accomplishments. Because Michael took the time to become good at one thing, lots of impressive achievements began to pile up for free. The same can happen for you. Model your extracurricular career after those of Kevin, Tom, Arnav, Geoffrey, and Michael. Focus on becoming very good at one thing. Have faith that this focus will not translate into a paltry, one-line activity list attached to your college application. The Complementary-Accomplishments Hypothesis says that your focused ability will be rewarded with a pile of complementary accomplishments that will be more impressive than any you could generate by spending more time spread over multiple unrelated projects.

As you go forth and ruthlessly cull your schedule in your quest to master a single skill, you can quell your undercommitment anxiety with the words of Matthew: "For unto every one that hath, more shall be given, and he shall have abundance."

9

When More Is Less

IN THE fall of 2008, I wrote a blog post about an overloaded high school senior. I discovered him on a popular college discussion bulletin board where he had anonymously posted his extracurricular and course schedules. He was seeking advice on how to reduce the intense stress in his life. "Quite frankly, I don't have room to breathe," he wrote. "I'm feeling the effects of it physically."

Below is his list of commitments. When you read it, you'll understand his woe:

* Costumer for a school play
* Plays three instruments
* Receives private language tutoring
* Heavy course load (5 AP courses in current semester)
* Member of the debate team
* Book fair organizer
* Multicultural fair organizer
* Secretary of the French club

* Member of the honor board
* Founded and runs his own club
* Founded and runs his own nonprofit

To some readers, this list will seem absurdly packed. To others, it will seem distressingly familiar. This same strategy is replicated tens of thousands of times each year by students hoping to gain admission to top schools. At its core is a simple idea: the more you do, the better.

However, my own instinctive response to reading his anonymous post was: "He's not going to get accepted into his reach schools." I knew nothing else about him—it was just a knee-jerk reaction to his schedule.

My blog readers experienced a similar reaction. A reader named Ryan commented: "All these people I know are filling their lives with . . . clubs, unimportant officer positions, etc. . . . All these students—valedictorians and 2,300+ SAT scorers included—are now being rejected by all the Ivy League schools." And he was not alone in this sentiment. There's just something about that long list of commitments that hits us—and presumably also admissions officers—the wrong way.

This vague, subjective feeling fascinates me because, logically speaking, adding more things to your schedule shouldn't hurt. As a high school student named David told me while attempting to justify a similarly overloaded lifestyle: "I would say that I probably [do] a bunch of unnecessary stuff, but I can handle it and it doesn't take a physical toll, so I'm good for now." He argued that, all things being equal, if you have the time to squeeze in one more club, then why not? It might not help much, but it doesn't seem that it could make things worse.

This sounds rational. Then again, when I read that list of activities, I still feel uneasy about the student. Something deeper must be going on.

The Laundry List Fallacy

I want to try a simple experiment. Imagine that the overloaded high school senior mentioned above drastically reduced his list from eleven commitments to the following two:

* Founded and runs his own club
* Founded and runs his own nonprofit

From an objective perspective, this edit should make his admission chances slightly worse. All I did was take his original list of commitments and then remove things. Yet for me, and for many students on whom I've tried this experiment, the drastically reduced list reads better. When only these two activities are described, I lose my knee-jerk reaction that this is a student on track for a rejection. Instead, I'm intrigued. I would want to find out more from his essays and recommendations before passing final judgment, but he definitely exudes a sense of potential interestingness that piques my curiosity.

Doing *more* things made this student seem *less* impressive. This idea is counterintuitive, but it arises often in the admissions process. When we see a long list of activities, we immediately think that this is an average student working as hard as possible to squeak past the acceptance threshold. In other words, that long, exhaustively constructed list shouts: *Warning! Grind at work!*

This effect is so common that I've captured it in its own hypothesis:

The Laundry List Hypothesis
Adding to your schedule an activity that could be replicated by any student willing to sign up and invest a reasonable amount of time in it can hurt your impressiveness. It follows that creating a laundry list of mediocre activities reduces your chances of college acceptance.

This hypothesis is hard for many students to accept. There's strong inertia pushing you to add just one more thing to your schedule. Fighting this force is difficult. It's much easier to default to the sentiments of David, who said, "I can handle it . . . I'm good for now." But the truth behind the Laundry List Hypothesis comes from more than just intuition. A pair of economists, working with a statistician, have spent the last half decade studying this effect in a variety of contexts. It's to their work that I turn your attention next.

The Honest Peacock

We begin our journey in the Sultanpur National Park, located about 35 kilometers outside New Delhi in Northern India. If you're lucky, among the dense shrubs and twisted trunks of the banyan groves, you might catch sight of the park's most valued resident: the Indian blue peacock. If you arrive in the late spring, during the birds' mating season, you'll likely see the males fan their famed ornamental tail feathers. The iridescent greens and blues of the feathers are adorned with eye-shaped spots. The whole display seems to shimmer as if seen through a heat haze— an effect produced by nano-sized structures in the barbules of the feathers that ricochet light waves back to our eyes in a chaotic pattern.

It's an amazing sight.

I've brought you on this ornithological detour because the peacock's plumage teaches an important lesson about a fascinating subject: how the most fit among us signal our brilliance to the rest of the world.

As you probably learned in school, peacocks use their elaborate feathers to attract mates. The better-looking the male's feathers, the better chance it has of attracting a female. Biologists have observed a wide variety of these feather displays, from stunningly fancy to paltry. Interestingly, the feathers seem to behave as what biologists call "honest signals." That is, they accurately describe the fitness of the animal to which they belong, which is a fancy way of saying that the better birds have better feathers. This basic observation, however, introduces a thorny question: Why didn't these birds evolve to lie? That is, why aren't all birds, regardless of their actual fitness, trying to grow the most elaborate possible feather displays? The most compelling explanation for this honesty was proposed in the late 1970s by the evolutionary biologist Richard Dawkins and his Oxford colleague, famed bird expert John R. Krebs. They argued that such signals evolved as an escalating "arms race" between predator and prey. In the case of the peacock, the more elaborate the bird's feathers the easier it is for a predator to find and eat it. Therefore, only the birds best able to escape from such a predator—that is, the healthiest and strongest birds—can risk growing an elaborate display. For a weak bird, such boasting would be suicide—the equivalent of hanging a dinner bell around its neck. Evolution, therefore, forges a link between a bird's strength and the elaborateness of its feathers. The signals are honest not because the animals are nice, or, as biologists used to think, because it's good for the species as a whole, but because it's evolution's best solution to the ongoing war between predator and prey—a by-product of a natural world that Tennyson famously called "red in tooth and claw."

This idea eventually expanded into its own field, known as signaling theory. It wasn't until 2002, however, that this theory first intersected with the world of college admissions. In that year, the economists Nick Feltovich and Rick Harbaugh, working with statistician Ted To, used signaling theory as the starting point for answering a simple but vexing question: Why don't the smart kids raise their hands more in class?

The Peacock in the Classroom

When considering the question posed by Feltovich, Harbaugh, and To, ignore the effects of peer pressure (i.e., that students fear it's uncool to look smart). These researchers were interested in the phenomenon occurring in classrooms where being smart was unambiguously good—for example, at an elite school. In such a setting, classical signaling theory says that the dumb kids can't risk raising their hand because they might get called on and give the wrong answer (the equivalent of the unfit bird growing elaborate plumage and then promptly being eaten). It follows that a student who confidently raises his or her hand at every opportunity must actually be smart; therefore the smart kids should constantly volunteer. But that is not what happens in real classrooms. Teachers report that the brightest students often seem to go out of their way to avoid offering an answer. The researchers set out to explain this observation, and ended up with a counterintuitive answer.

Feltovich, Harbaugh, and To took the classical signaling theory model and added a new twist: a *side channel* that sends extra information about the signaler. The important property of the side channel is that the signaler can't control it. In the world of the peacocks, for example, fights between male birds act like a side channel that's more likely to send positive information about better birds. Presumably, winning a fight sends a good signal about a bird's strength to the watching female birds. A male bird can't choose in advance how a fight will turn out, but the stronger he is, the better the chance that he will win.

When the researchers applied this new model to the classroom setting, they reasoned that the smarter the student, the higher the chance that her classmates will have heard about her brainpower indirectly through a side channel—perhaps hallway gossip or overheard conversations. The researchers then captured this idea in a precise mathematical model to deduce the best strategy for the smart students to signal good things about themselves. To their happy surprise, the answer matched what was observed in real classrooms: the best strategy for the smart kids to signal their intelligence is to rarely answer questions.

When you deconstruct the mathematics driving this result, a simple explanation emerges. The *medium-ability* students have to signal their skill by answering lots of questions. They can't rely on the side channel to convey information about their smarts, as they aren't actually smart enough for this to be very likely. Their big fear is that if they don't answer questions and the side channel fails to send something positive, they'll appear indistinguishable from the *low-ability* students (who never volunteer answers or expect anything good about their intelligence to be conveyed through the side channel). It's better to get a few questions wrong and be accurately labeled as medium-ability than it is to be mistaken for low-ability.

The *high-ability* students, by contrast, are confident that the side channel will send positive information about their intelligence. That is, they assume their reputation precedes them into the classroom. Thus their best strategy to differentiate themselves from the medium-ability students is to rarely answer questions. They deploy this strategy exactly because the medium-ability students can't risk it. Put another way, only a student who is truly confident about her skills can afford to avoid showing them off.

The researchers named this strategy *countersignaling* because of its counterintuitive conclusion that *not* signaling can sometimes be the best signal of all. They soon discovered a variety of settings in which their theory explained observed behavior. In a job interview, for example, if you're a top candidate, the theory says it's best not to brag about your grades. Only an applicant truly confident that his reputation for smarts precedes him—for example, in his references—can risk not bragging. Therefore, if you don't make a point of mentioning that you're Phi Beta Kappa, you'll come across as even smarter. Similarly, for a new professor, the better the school where you teach, the less need you have to brag about your PhD—the reputation of the school acts as a side channel that passes along positive information about your credentials. This last prediction was verified in an elegant experiment in which the researchers called the voice mail of professors in the California public university system. As predicted, the better the school's ranking, the less likely they were to hear "you've reached *Doctor* . . ." start the voice mail greeting.

The Peacock in the Admissions Process

The theory of countersignaling can help explain the Laundry List Hypothesis. Consider the extracurricular activity list you attach to your college application. Every item on this list is a signal of your admissions fitness. You control these signals by choosing what to join. In addition, we can imagine a side channel that is out of your control. In admissions, this side channel might include your recommendations and the report generated by your student interviewer. It might also include your awards and your essay—the best, most interesting students' essays tend to emanate something special. As the theory would have it, the better the student, the more likely that this side channel will say something good about him.

The theory of countersignaling says that the medium-ability applicants should include long activity lists in their applications. They can't trust that their side channel will provide a strong endorsement, so they need to send lots of positive signals on the channel they do control: their extracurriculars. If they don't, they risk appearing indistinguishable from the automatically rejected low-ability applicants. (The assumption here is that the low-ability applicants will always have sparse activity lists, and their side channel will rarely say something good about them.)

The high-ability applicants, by contrast, can trust that their side channel will convey great things. With this in mind, to differentiate themselves from the medium-ability applicants they should send fewer positive signals by way of their activities list. Put another way, the top applicants trust that their reputation as stars precedes them, so they can confidently avoid the mediocre activities that any diligent students could replicate.

This theory explains our reaction to the student from the beginning of this chapter. His long list of activities turned us off because it matched the best strategy for a medium-ability applicant. It made him seem like an average student doing everything possible to try to squeeze himself just above the acceptance threshold. By contrast, the reduced version of his activity list matched what we might expect from a high-ability applicant— the two items it included were impressive enough to convince us that his side channel would likely add something positive. This is why we felt intrigued by his potential.

The theory of countersignaling also explains a surprising discovery I made while researching this book: many students who get accepted into top colleges actually omit activities from their applications. For example, Jessica, whom you met in Part 1, and Maneesh, about whom you'll learn more in Part 3, both admitted that they left off activities. The theory also explains why students like Michael Silverman, who had only a small number of highly focused accomplishments on his résumé, did so well during the admissions process. The short activity lists of these students match the template for a high-ability applicant.

The theory of countersignaling provides my final argument for the law of focus. Whereas the previous two chapters described the impressiveness that is generated by doing something very well, this chapter describes the impressiveness lost by the opposing strategy of doing many things kind of well. It leads us to the surprising conclusion that when it comes to college admissions, sometimes less is more.

In the playbook section that follows, I provide some practical advice for following this law. I begin by helping you identify your focused pursuits. Once these pursuits are identified, the task of restricting your attention to them is easy. More difficult, however, is actually mastering them. It's surprisingly common for students to spend a lot of time on an activity without gaining much ability. With this in mind, I next walk you through what I call the art of becoming good. I conclude with advice for maintaining the focused life over the long run. If you combine a commitment to focus with the strategies ahead, you'll ensure yourself a quick transition onto a relaxed superstar trajectory.

Part 2

Playbook

THE LAW of focus asks that you restrict your attention to a small number of pursuits that you stick with throughout your high school career. Eventually this focus should lead to mastery, which acts like a shot of steroids into your impressiveness muscles. In practice, however, this process is not always so straightforward. First you face the challenge of identifying *what to focus on*. I've met many students who were paralyzed with indecision due to their fear that they might choose the wrong pursuit. Assuming you overcome this fear, and are able to identify the target of your focus, there's still no guarantee that simply restricting your attention will lead to the mastery that allows the Superstar Effect and Matthew Effect to work their magic. Spending time on something is not synonymous with becoming good at it. And once you've adopted the focused lifestyle, the small responsibilities of daily life have a way of nudging you back toward a more cluttered existence. The focused student must be vigilant about fighting this *complexity creep*.

This playbook addresses these concerns. To simplify the

presentation, I've divided it into three sections. The first section provides straightforward advice for identifying a focus. The next section contains a series of subsections dedicated to what I call *the art of becoming good*. Mastering a skill is nontrivial. These subsections will teach you the strategies you need to conquer this art. The final section of the playbook concerns maintaining the focused life. Drawing inspiration from one of history's greatest scientists, I outline a habit that will keep your attention uncluttered.

Identifying a Focus

I frequently preach the gospel of focus on my student advice blog. On the day that I'm editing this chapter (August 19, 2009), half of the articles on my home page emphasize the idea that students should master a small number of things. Jose Quesada, founder of the popular Academic Productivity site, recently called this topic the "leitmotiv" of my blogging.* And he's right. I mention the idea so often that many of my readers have started to preface their e-mailed questions with some variation of the following disclaimer: "I know you're going to tell me that I should be doing less things, but . . ."

As you may imagine, therefore, I receive a lot of feedback on this topic—not all of it positive. A reader named Basu, for example, recently commented: "While I certainly agree with the basic idea of focusing your effort, I think it's hard to determine . . . what [this] one 'item' is. . . . Simply doing the same things as other people, even if you do them well, might not be enough." Another reader noted: "I can see the appeal of focusing on a few things; however, I instead try to focus on becoming a really good learner and then apply that skill to become as multifaceted as possible." Along the same lines, several readers recently

---

*SAT Word Alert: *leitmotiv*—a recurrent theme.

commented in support of the idea that students should experiment with lots of endeavors and postpone committing to one until college graduation. As one of these students concluded: "To me, [being a student] should be about expanding identity, and part of that is to try many, many things and fail at most of them." Behind these comments I detect a common fear: "What if I choose the wrong thing to focus on?" It is often coupled with this concern: "If I prune my activities too soon, I might miss out on my *true calling*." I want to address this fear and convince you that choosing a focus is easier and less risky than you might think.

When I counsel students on this topic, I begin by noting that underscheduling must precede focus. As I argued in Part 1 of this book, deep interests—pursuits that you return to voluntarily, again and again, whenever you have free time—are near magical in their ability to transform your life from mediocre to interesting. I dedicated many pages in the Part 1 playbook to teaching you how to open your schedule and expose yourself to enough random inputs that a deep interest can arise naturally. (As you'll recall, the key lesson of this part was that such interests cannot be forced or faked; you have to live a lifestyle conducive to their development.)

My advice for identifying a focus, therefore, is to start by forming a deep interest. You can then focus your attention on pursuits related to this deep interest. Because the pursuit is based on something deep, you can be assured that your ability to focus on it will remain strong throughout your student career. On a practical level, it would be wasteful to segregate the advice in Part 1 from that in Part 2. If you used your deep interests only to generate interestingness, and then focused on an unrelated pursuit to generate the Superstar Effect and Matthew Effect, you'd be doubling your efforts. By combining the two, you retain the benefits of both strategies while investing less overall effort.

This first answer is not always enough to calm students' fears.

Some might agree that a deep-interest-generated pursuit will provide them with the interestingness factor promoted in Part 1, but they worry that if this interest doesn't coincide with one of their "natural talents," they may never reach the level of skill needed for the benefits of the law of focus to take effect. You may have noticed that I placed "natural talents" in quotation marks. This takes us to the crux of my second answer: the idea that such talents exist is overrated.

To start, let's take a look at ourselves in the proverbial mirror. American society is enamored with the idea of natural ability. In a study conducted by Sun Xuhua of the Chinese University of Hong Kong, for example, a cohort of Chinese and American students, from the tenth and eleventh grades, filled out questionnaires on their attitudes about math. The results showed a striking difference between the two cultures. "Eastern societies tend to highly value effort, perseverance, and hard work," concluded Sun, "whereas Western counterparts tend to view mathematical ability and creativity as the more important contributing factors for success." That is, we in the West think that math talent is something you're born with, while people in the East see it as a skill, like any other, that can be developed through practice. My own experiences match these results. When I tell Americans I have a PhD in theoretical computer science from MIT, for example, they quickly conjure up images of *Good Will Hunting*–style geniuses who solve equations by glancing at a chalkboard. (I wish.) Moving beyond math, our culture holds a similar belief about most pursuits, from sports to the arts: you have to match your effort to your natural talents to become great.

A growing body of research, however, challenges this mind-set. To return to my personal experience, I've discovered that most of the people I work with at MIT validate the Eastern model. Maybe early in their lives they showed a slight aptitude for math that was recognized and that built their confidence, but the amazing skills they wield today as professional researchers come from an amazing amount of practice. To give another example, a common phenomenon at universities is for undergraduates to feel that their grad student teaching assistants are smarter than they are ("He solves these homework problems so easily!"), while the grad students feel that the professors have an even more superior intellect ("She solves these open research problems so easily!"). This effect doesn't highlight a hierarchy of natural ability. It's more easily explained by differences in experience—the longer you've worked in a field, the better you get.

Another compelling argument for this perspective comes from the 2008 book *Talent Is Overrated*, written by Geoff Colvin, a senior editor at *Fortune*. Colvin draws on the growing scientific consensus that investing *the right type* of practice on a focused pursuit is more important than natural ability when it comes to becoming a star performer.

"We assume that Mozart was born with an astounding gift for music, just as Warren Buffett carries the gene for making brilliant investments," says Colvin. "The trouble is, scientific evidence doesn't support the notion that specific natural talents make great performers—and such talents may not even exist."

The upside of this consensus is that it removes the pressure from your choice of a focused pursuit. According to Colvin, and the scientists he cites, there's probably *no* right pursuit that best matches some innate talent. You can master almost *any* pursuit you choose, so long as you practice it in the right sort of way. (Not coincidentally, the playbook sections that follow will teach you the secrets to this optimal practice.) With this in mind, you can relax and let your deep interests guide you to something that piques your curiosity. You can then focus your attention in this single direction, free from worries about matching your endeavors to some mythical natural talent. You don't need a perfect pursuit, just one that's good enough to hold your attention. As I like to conclude when advising focus-averse students, the only wrong choice when it comes to focusing is choosing not to focus at all.

The Art of Becoming Good

John is good at what he does. *Really good*. When he applied to Princeton, where he now studies, he was the valedictorian of his class. He also had perfect SAT scores and was the first-chair violinist in his school's orchestra.

If you get to know John, as I have over the past year, it soon becomes apparent that he's a living incarnation of the law of focus. His high school world consisted entirely of academics and the violin—and he eventually got so good at both that the resulting Superstar Effect had admissions officers scrambling to accept him. He also reaped the benefits of the Matthew Effect. John says that his intense focus on improving his academic abilities led to his top SAT scores, high GPA, and the embarrassment of academic awards and honors he eventually accrued. Similarly, his ability as a violinist spawned impressive opportunities. In addition to earning a seat in his county orchestra, he founded a club dedicated to bringing live music into local nursing homes. These accomplishments didn't require much time, but instead arose naturally given his leadership position in the orchestra. Finally, countersignaling undoubtedly played a role in John's rise to stardom. With an extracurricular résumé focused on such a small number of pursuits, he escaped the stigma of sending too many signals.*

I hope that you agree by now that mastering a small number of

---

* Keep in mind that the targets of John's focus—academics and violin playing—were risky, as they both have well-defined competitive structures and are difficult to master. It's because of this difficulty that John's story proves so useful to our purposes here. His tactics for becoming good must have been very effective if he rose to the top in these demanding pursuits.

pursuits generates huge rewards—as it did for John. But becoming good is not always easy. Consider John's accomplishments. You might maintain that even if you focused *all* of your attention on a small number of pursuits, you would still fall short of John's level of success. When I dove deeper into John's story, however, it became clear that what makes him special is not an abundance of brains or an innate rapport with the violin. Instead, the driving force behind his successes was his mastery of the art of becoming good. He wasn't content to simply spend time on these pursuits. He wanted to spend *the right kind of time*—hours that were carefully crafted to improve his abilities as fast as possible. In the three sections that follow, I want to convince you that his level of success is available to most students—if you know what you're doing.

The Art of Becoming Good, Part 1: The Goodness Paradox

When I was researching my book *How to Become a Straight-A Student*, I noticed an intriguing paradox. It became clear that most students *think* they know how to earn excellent grades, yet few students actually reach this goal. When they try to improve their performance, they deploy the techniques they assume are right (study longer and harder), and then, when they fail to see much improvement, they concoct various excuses for their failure ("I know how to get better grades, but I would have to give up my social life to have enough time to achieve this goal!"). It rarely crosses their minds that perhaps their strategy is to blame.

As I continued my research for *Straight-A*, I decided to discard the assumptions I held about studying and instead start from scratch. I found fifty college students, from a variety of schools and majors, who actually achieved the goal of scoring great grades. I then asked them how they did it. As fans of that book know, the techniques I uncovered differ significantly from the study-longer-and-harder strategy most students think is right.

For example, most students study in long stretches at night, usually starting after dinner. Top-scoring students, by contrast, tend to study in short bursts throughout the morning and afternoon. Most students review by reading over their notes, while top students prefer to recall ideas out loud, as if lecturing an imaginary class. And so on. Best of all, the techniques I uncovered tend to require less time and produce better results.

What struck me about this experience was that most students would be better off if they simply assumed they knew nothing about getting good grades. It's their certainty that prevents them from discovering the simpler, more time-effective techniques that actually work.

To begin our study of the art of becoming good, I want to offer this general observation:

The Goodness Paradox
Most people assume they know how to become good. Yet most are not good at anything.

The purpose of *the goodness paradox* is to get you questioning the assumptions you hold about how to become better at a particular pursuit. These assumptions, if left unchallenged, might become a roadblock preventing actual progress. I argue that the best strategy for becoming good is the strategy I deployed for *Straight-A*: Ignore what you think is right and go ask people who are already good. Put another way, assume you know *nothing* about your area of focus. Instead, make it your mission to learn from those who do.

Let's return to John for a moment and see how he made use of this strategy. He entered a large public high school in Texas having done "reasonably well" in junior high, but he was far from being an academic standout. "I entered high school with the same mentality as junior high: I would take difficult classes and try to do well in them," he recalls. At the end of his freshman year, however, he discovered that through a combination of luck, hard studying, and the lack of rigor in freshman courses, his GPA ranked him fourteenth in his class. "Surprised at my ranking, I decided that I would make a go at getting into a good college," John says. Most students in this situation would jump into a strategy of harder work and less sleep, driven by the assumption that they know what it takes to do better academically.

Not John.

"I made up my mind to learn from students who were older than me," he told me. "I met the valedictorian and the salutatorian of the tenth grade, and I asked them for advice." He learned two key ideas from these interviews. First, he should find students who are the best in his class in a *specific subject*—not necessarily best overall—and learn from them about how to master that subject. Second, he should avoid other students who are also competing to have the best overall GPA, to keep from getting sucked into their competitive world.

John took this advice to heart. His writing was weaker than his quantitative skills, for example, so he introduced himself to a girl in his English class who was known as the best writer of their year. He asked her to help him learn how to write better. "She genuinely liked writing," John recalls. "She was reading novels all the time." Soon he began to analyze her essays to see what made them shine. He also asked her to look over the essays he wrote to see where they fell short. He and the girl had deep conversations about reading and the art of writing, and John's skills improved at a rapid pace. In return for this assistance, he helped her with the subjects he was already good at, like math.

Most students in John's situation would either avoid English classes or hope that a combination of increased study time plus grade grubbing would generate the needed marks. By contrast,

John put himself at the feet of the best and gave himself a crash course in becoming a better writer. Top grades in these courses came easily after these lessons.

He followed the same approach for taming the SAT. "I talked to a friend who had scored a 1600," John told me. "He said to buy the Barron's prep book and the book of real tests published by the College Board. They have the best sample questions." Following his friend's advice, he ignored fancy test strategies and focused exclusively on taking practice tests and memorizing vocabulary words. "When I took the practice tests and graded them, I would rework the problems I had missed, without looking at the explanations at the back. . . . This is really the best way to learn." After a while, however, his performance hit a plateau. Discussing this issue with his friend, he discovered that the top scorers learn to solve the easier math problems in their head—leaving enough time free to check answers and weed out careless mistakes. (Interestingly, time management, more so than raw smarts, seems to be what separates high scores from perfect scores on these tests.) Using this knowledge, John recruited his sister to quiz him out loud on sample problems so that he could practice solving them quickly in his head. "I wanted the math section to become instinctive," he said.

John deployed similar tactics with his violin playing. "A big part of orchestra was to make sure that I understood specifically where I was messing up," he told me. "After every 'chair test'—where students perform live in front of the class for the conductor—I would ask the conductor for written comments. I would then come home after school to ensure that I understood which part I was messing up on." When the conductor told him that he was having pacing trouble, for example, he spent that same evening with a metronome until the problem was solved.

What fascinates me about John is that he has no patience for the idea of natural talent. He entered high school as an above-average, but not stellar, student who was a decent, but not great, violin player. Instead of setting out on a quest to discover his true calling, John decided to get good at the traits he thought would be most important. (Not surprising, he recently revealed to me that he's a big fan of Geoff Colvin's book.) To begin his quest toward this goal, John embraced the truth revealed by the goodness paradox: in every pursuit he eventually mastered, he started by ignoring his own assumptions and going straight to the experts.

You should follow John's example in your own effort to become good. Once you've decided *where* to focus, start with a blank slate. Don't dive in under the assumption that you know what to do. Find the experts at your school. Learn from them. The small time investment required to figure out how to become good will pay for itself many times over.

The Art of Becoming Good, Part 2: The Immersion Hypothesis
John's story taught us that the first step to becoming good is avoiding the temptation to jump right in and start flailing forward. But once you've done this research, what comes next? To answer this question, I want to return to John's story and consider his rise from an average violin player to concert master.

"There were players who were better than me, so I tried to stand out in other ways," John told me. "I demonstrated that I was devoted to the orchestra in more than just performing. I volunteered at orchestra fund-raisers and listened to tons of classical music. I accompanied my practice with books about composers. It was fascinating—I became a fan of less well-known composers like Kabalevsky and Berg. I immersed myself in the world of classical music."

The key word from John's experience is *immersion*. Once you have chosen a pursuit to master, and have sought expert advice about how to proceed, dedicate yourself completely to the world of that pursuit. Becoming excellent is not a casual enterprise. That nerdy kid from your high school who won all of those robotics competitions, and then got into MIT, probably lived and breathed robotics—it wasn't just an isolated activity on a long list of unrelated commitments. To give another example, recall the girl who helped John become a better writer. He noted that she read lots of novels on her own time and liked to write for fun. This immersion helped earn her the status as the class's top English student.

I capture this general idea with the following hypothesis:

The Immersion Hypothesis
The more you immerse yourself in the world surrounding an activity, the more success with the activity you'll experience.

There are three explanations for why this hypothesis holds true. The first concerns commitment. When you dedicate a significant portion of your extracurricular time to a single field, you're signaling true commitment to yourself. Without this commitment, your mind has a way of throwing up obstacles to your progress. If it doesn't trust that you *really* want to do this, it will defend against potentially wasted effort with procrastination and excuses. If John hadn't surrounded himself with the world of classical music, for example, but instead just tried to force himself to practice hard for a few hours every day, he would have faced a tough mental battle. When he instead immersed himself in that world—listening to music, attending performances, reading books about composers—practicing became a natural part of his larger commitment to music. Looking back on this immersion, John agrees, noting: "It was a good way to keep up my motivation."

The second explanation concerns the aggregation of many

small bursts of effort. When you're immersed in a world, you end up investing lots of small chunks of time toward improving your craft—even if you don't always realize it. Over time, these can add up to a significant amount of extra practice. To return to John's example, the time he spent listening to music, reading about composers, chatting with the conductor, and in general being around music and people who play music, probably provided lots of micro-boosts to his knowledge of violin playing. The boosts eventually added up to a significant edge over a player who practices in isolation.

The final explanation concerns opportunity. The more you're immersed in a world, the greater the probability that you'll stumble into opportunities to increase your ability. This too proved true in John's story. Because of his immersion in everything having to do with classical music, he eventually befriended some players from his county's symphony orchestra. "I went to the concerts, got to know the director, and polished one piece again and again, until it was perfect for auditions," John recalls. Eventually, John performed the piece for the conductor, who then agreed to let John join.

"I was back in the second violin section," John admits, "but it was a blast to be able to play with adults." More important, playing at this level forced John to improve his technique beyond what he was exposed to in the high school orchestra.

The Immersion Hypothesis predicts that good things come from involving yourself in the many small activities and interests surrounding the pursuit you want to master. Of course, when deploying this strategy you must keep the law of focus in mind. You can afford to immerse yourself in one or at most two different fields before the time demands become too intense to sustain. Start by whittling down your interests to a small number of focused pursuits; then immerse yourself in their world.

The Art of Becoming Good, Part 3: The Leveraged-Ability Hypothesis
We've arrived at the final part of our investigation into the art of becoming good. The previous parts taught you to learn from the experts and then immerse yourself in the pursuit. This final part addresses a more subtle topic: how to increase your *perceived* ability. Recall that the effects of the law of focus described throughout Part 2 hold once you're unambiguously recognized as being very good at something. Therefore, your perceived ability is as important as your actual ability. We begin, as before, with John's story.

"My junior year, I became first chair of my school's orchestra," John told me. "I then leveraged this accomplishment to start a club, the Nursing Home Orchestra Performance Group. Basically, the members of the orchestra would get together to play at local nursing homes."

There are two things to note about this act of leverage. First, the club wasn't a huge time commitment, as John admits: "The total time to set this up was about twelve hours; it was both fun and easy." Second, it made John *appear* to be even better at music. On his résumé he could list that he was "the director of a performance group." This accomplishment, of course, signals talent.

To pull this off, however, John had to first pass a relatively high threshold of ability. He was able to start this organization only because he was already the concert master, and therefore the de facto student leader, of his orchestra. He would've had much more difficulty organizing the group as a freshman or sophomore with little standing. The key point to notice, therefore, is that he leveraged his ability, once it began to develop, to create opportunities that were unavailable to those without his level of skill. As with the performance group John started, these types of leveraged opportunities typically boost your perceived ability without requiring an excessive time investment—making them a perfect match for the focused lifestyle. (This phenomenon is one of the many specific realizations of the general Matthew Effect.)

For another example, consider Michael Silverman. He leveraged his ability in doing sustainability projects to set up a classroom program to teach younger students about green energy. Practically, this involved installing a Web interface that allowed students to track the power generated by the solar panels he installed on the school's maintenance shed. This task wasn't particularly time consuming (the power company provided the equipment and software), and it certainly boosted Michael's perceived ability as a sustainability guru. The opportunity was available to him, however, only because of his previous accomplishments in the field.

This phenomenon is common enough to warrant its own hypothesis:

> **The Leveraged-Ability Hypothesis**
> Once you pass a certain threshold of skill in a field, you'll encounter many opportunities for related activities that will improve your perceived ability without requiring an excessive time commitment.

John took advantage of this reality. So did Michael Silverman. And you can too. Once you begin to become good at your focused pursuit, leverage your burgeoning talent to find the easy opportunities that enhance your image as a star.

Maintaining Focus

Between the years 1912 and 1915, Albert Einstein was a focused man. His earlier work on his special theory of relativity and the quantization of light, among other topics, was starting to gain him notice. Einstein had left the Swiss patent office, and after short stints as a professor in Germany and Prague, ended up, in 1912, at the ETH Institute in Zurich. Once there, he worked with the mathematician Marcel Grossman and soon became convinced that if he applied the non-Euclidean math studied by Grossman to his own work on relativity, he could generalize the theory to account for gravity. This advance would be huge—an effective revision to the fundamental laws of Nature.

With a clear focus identified, Einstein set to work.

Between 1912 and 1915, the young scientist became increasingly obsessed in his push to formalize general relativity. As revealed by several sources, including his recently released letters, he worked so hard that his marriage became strained and his hair turned white from the stress. But he got it done. In 1915 he published his full theory. It stands today as one of the greatest scientific accomplishments—if not the single greatest—of the twentieth century.

Einstein's story provides a canonical example of the focused lifestyle. His focused pursuit was theoretical physics. His project within this pursuit was generalizing his special theory of relativity. By pointing his prodigious energies toward this project, he generated massively important results. In a perfect world, we would all be Einsteins—our small number of focused pursuits would yield a small number of clearly defined projects on which we could focus our attention like a laser beam. Reality, however, is often much messier.

The big problem is that we don't know in advance which project might turn out to be our own theory of relativity, and which projects are dead ends. Because of this, most ambitious students I know tend to follow a different strategy. They sow lots of project seeds related to their small number of focused pursuits. They e-mail people, read related books and articles, commit to minor projects, set up meetings, and send out feelers to friends and connections regarding their latest brainstorm—the type of exploration described in the Part 1 playbook. They don't know which seed will ultimately take root and grow into something important, so by planting many, they expose themselves to enough randomness to maximize their eventual chance of stumbling into the *right* project.

My entrance into the world of writing, for example, followed this approach. Over the summer following my freshman year of college, I decided to make writing one of my focused pursuits. I didn't know the best project to get started in this field, so I tried lots of different things. Some of my first steps were to submit op-ed pieces to the student newspaper and start working on a book proposal for an advice-guide idea. The book proposal was a dead end at the time, but my first two op-ed pieces were published. This led me to apply to become a columnist for the school newspaper. Not one for self-seriousness, I gravitated toward a humorous writing style, and this led me to join, and eventually lead, the campus humor magazine. Dozens of similar projects followed. Some paid off; others fizzled. But my writing ability continued to grow, as did my knowledge of the field. It wasn't until the summer after my junior year, when I signed the contract for my first book, *How to Win at College*, that I was able to develop a clear vision of how a professional writing career could unfold—a vision I've been following ever since. Looking back, I see that it required a lot of experimentation to get to the place where I could focus on a small number of projects with confidence.

As I discovered, the main difficulty with the sow-lots-of-seeds method is that so many of the seeds grow into weeds—time-consuming projects that impede your path to mastery. (My early book proposal idea is one such example.) To maintain an Einstein-style focused lifestyle, therefore, it's crucial to learn how to pull these weeds before they overwhelm the projects that have a chance of meaningful success. If you fail in your weeding, your attempts to stay focused will be thwarted as you find yourself rushing from obligation to obligation, none of which is really advancing your skill. Below, I offer a simple strategy to help you hone your ability to keep your project garden weeded. I call this method *the productivity purge*.

The Productivity Purge

This method consists of five steps:

1. At the beginning of each semester, label a sheet of paper with the names of your focused pursuits. Having one or two pursuits is optimal. Three is doable if you happen to have an abundance of free time. If you have more than three pursuits, however, then you need to make some hard choices. Because not every project in your life is tied to a big-picture pursuit (for example, learning to play guitar), add the label "extra" to the sheet to capture these outliers.

2. Under each label list all of the related projects currently in progress. The word "project," in this context, refers to anything that requires a regular time commitment.

3. For each list, put a star next to the *one or two projects* that you think have the greatest chance of returning rewards. For the focused-pursuit lists, "rewards" refers to advances in your ability. For the "extra" list, however, you can star the one or two projects that you enjoy the most.

4. Next, consider the nonstarred projects that remain on the list. Identify those that you could stop working on right away with no serious consequences. Cross these out and do no further work on them. For each of the projects still left unmarked (i.e., they are neither starred nor crossed out), come up with a one-to-two-week "crunch plan" for finalizing and dispatching them. For example, maybe one

of the unmarked projects is a commitment to the school newspaper, which you now recognize as unimportant to advancing you focused pursuits. Your crunch plan for shutting down this project might involve finishing the article you're currently assigned, and then telling the editor that you can't take on additional articles this semester due to an abundance of other stuff in your life.

5. Once you complete your crunch plans you'll be left with only a small number of important projects for each of your focused pursuits, plus a couple of enjoyable projects left under your "extra" label. At this point, you have *purged* your schedule of all but the small number of contenders that have the best chance of becoming your own theory of relativity.

The productivity purge is a great way to maintain a focused lifestyle. By conducting one of these purges at least a few times a year, you'll keep your attention on what's important while avoiding the need to obsess over your schedule on a daily basis. To this day, I do a productivity purge once a month in order to balance my need to experiment with my need for an uncluttered life. The method has worked wonders for me. It will for you too.

Pulling It All Together

You probably began the Part 2 playbook convinced of the power of focus but unsure of how to make focus a reality in your own life. It's easy to decide to restrict your attention to a few targets, but it's a whole different challenge to put the decision into practice. This playbook has addressed that challenge.

The first section of the playbook tackled the fundamental question, What should I focus on? I told you to use your deep interests, described in Part 1 of the book, to guide you toward your focused pursuits. I also argued that you can ignore your fear of choosing the wrong focus, as most likely there's no perfect focus out there waiting for you to discover. In the second section, I used the story of John, the talented Princeton student, to guide you through the subtle art of becoming good at a pursuit once you've decided to direct your attention toward it. You learned about questioning your assumptions, immersing yourself in the world, and then leveraging your ability, once it begins to grow, to increase your perceived skills. With these tactics under your belt, the final challenge was to ensure that your pursuits didn't generate too many projects, which could impede meaningful progress. I answered this challenge, in the third section, with the productivity-purge method, a simple technique for keeping your project garden thriving.

Even with these strategies, you still might find your transition into the focused life difficult. Your choice of pursuits, for example, might need to be defined more clearly. You might struggle to make progress or to find the right projects to tackle. Don't worry. Focus is a practiced skill. Most students have trouble when first switching to this way of doing things, but it does get easier over time. You'll improve at defining your pursuits and become more adept at identifying the related projects that will generate the best returns. So have patience. Getting started is the hard part—once your momentum builds, you'll look back with disdainful wonder at the cluttered and unfocused life you used to live.

Part 3

The Law of Innovation

Pursue accomplishments that are hard to explain, not hard to do.

The law of innovation will transform your understanding of impressiveness. Most students think they know what makes an accomplishment stand out. If asked, they would say that the accomplishment must demonstrate hard work and talent. The law of innovation, by contrast, highlights the surprising importance of a different factor: how hard an accomplishment is to explain. That is, if I can't simulate in my mind how you did what you did, I'm going to consider you impressive—regardless of the actual difficulty of your feat.

Consider the following two students. The first served on a youth commission for the United Nations and the second is the president of his high school class. Who impresses you more? Almost everyone I've asked this question chooses the first student. But why is he more impressive? It's not because he worked harder or had more talent than the class president. The student I based this example on, about whom you'll hear more in the playbook, stumbled into the UN opportunity accidentally. The awe you feel reflects the fact that you have no idea how a high school student ends up working with the world's most important governing body. Because the path to becoming student body president, by contrast, is well understood, this accomplishment does not generate a similar impressiveness bonus. The crucial observation here is that whether or not something is *hard to explain* has little connection to whether or not it's *hard to do*. Relaxed superstars, understanding this fact, know how to pump up their impressiveness without sacrificing massive amounts of time.

In the chapters that follow, I explore this curious effect—from the science that explains it to the rules that describe where it applies. Along the way I'll have you meet three relaxed superstars who used the law of innovation to gain acceptance to their dream schools. You'll hear their stories, learn exactly how they got involved in their innovative pursuits, and then discover how you can follow a similar path.

10

The Laziest Student at Bella Vista High

ON A generically sunny California morning, in the fall of 2004, an unexpected event transpired: Maneesh Sethi, the self-described "laziest student at Bella Vista High School," was admitted into Stanford University.

Maneesh isn't lazy in the usual pejorative sense. He appreciates impressive accomplishments and has racked up a few of his own. It's just that he has no tolerance for crowded schedules, all-nighters, or any other sources of mind-numbing work marathons. Perhaps it's an attention-deficit disorder or a long-repressed phobia, but no matter how you describe it, the conclusion is clear: Maneesh Sethi is constitutionally incapable of being a grind.

"There are two types of overachievers," he explained to me when we first met. "Type As, who do massive amounts of work, and type Bs, who get type As to do their work for them. I was a type B."

When I asked Maneesh to send me a typical day's schedule from his senior year of high school, he sent one in which the hours from 11 a.m. to 3 p.m. were labeled as follows: "Done with school; hang out with friends, read, or more likely browse on the computer." (Maneesh and his friends had somehow convinced the administration to let them leave school before lunch.) In a similar spirit of ultrarelaxation, Maneesh described the period from 5 p.m. to 9 p.m. as time to "zone out."

Maneesh wasn't activity-phobic. In fact, he was involved with quite a few clubs off and on throughout high school. But he shunned activities that demanded serious time commitments.

"I guess at some point I had to physically do some work for these activities," Maneesh admitted. "But a lot of the clubs were jokes."

After a moment of consideration, he added: "A few were actual jokes. I started the math club just so I could get money from the school to give away free pie on Pi Day. That was the focus of the club." He laughed at the memory. "We never did a single math activity."

When I asked him to add up the total work time required by his extracurricular commitments, he responded: "I really don't remember spending more than two to five hours per week for everything all together."

There were, however, some isolated exceptions to this no-work rule. As a junior, Maneesh launched a literary journal featuring pieces written by students from area high schools. This required him to find funding and to travel between the schools, pitching the idea and soliciting submissions. The first edition came out during his junior year and the second during his senior year. The journal was well received in the district.

Work-averse Maneesh describes this as one of his biggest endeavors as a student. He recalls that the journal required two months of attention during his junior year and two months of attention during his senior year. During each two-month stretch, the final two weeks were the only hard ones. "In total, the journal generated about four hard weeks over my entire high school career," he concluded. To Maneesh this may have seemed demanding. To the typical elite applicant, however, four hard weeks out of four years is a walk in the park.

The second exception to his no-work rule was the fact that Maneesh played in a rock band between the ages of thirteen and sixteen. The band performed locally and was popular. This endeavor certainly required effort, but nothing overwhelming. Maneesh would practice his guitar frequently, and there were band practices most weeks. But as he summarizes, "It was never a real time sink."

The above reads like the résumé of a talented but underachieving high school student. You might expect that Maneesh would have no problem gaining admittance to a solid college (his grades and SAT scores were very good), but elite institutions like Stanford should have been out of his reach. Off-and-on club memberships, the literary journal, the rock band: these are all fine, but they don't add up to the type of superstar achievement that can gain admittance to a school with a 10 percent acceptance rate.

But Maneesh did get in—to every school where he applied, including Stanford and Berkeley. Something interesting must be going on here.

From Rocking to Writing

I have a confession. I changed one key fact about Maneesh's high school experience. He *didn't* play in a rock band. Instead, at the age of sixteen he published a book titled *Computer Game Programming for Teens*. The title sold well in America, at one point hitting number sixteen on the amazon.com bestseller list. It also sold well abroad. (For reasons unknown, it was a hit in Poland.) The success landed Maneesh a brief recurring segment on a show airing on the teen-oriented TechTV cable channel, where he answered viewer questions about game programming.

When I make this substitution, Maneesh's Stanford acceptance suddenly slides into focus. "Of course he got in," you think, "he wrote a bestselling book and was a TV personality!" Take a moment, however, to question this shift in your feelings. Why is writing a book substantially more impressive than playing in a popular local rock band? As I mentioned in the opening in Part 3, when I ask students what makes an activity impressive, they tend to circle back to responses such as hard work and talent. But does this apply here? Maneesh's example challenges these assumptions.

I'll start with hard work. Maneesh wrote his book over a period of two years. In fact, he was more than a year late handing in the manuscript due to his inability to do large amounts of writing all at once. Maneesh wrote when he had the time and energy—he estimates that he averaged only two hours of writing per week. The earlier quote about the rock band never being "a real time sink" was something Maneesh actually said about writing the book. In other words, playing in a rock band probably requires more hard work than Maneesh invested in his book. (As the former guitar player for a high school rock band, and the author of multiple books, I can base this claim on my own experience. Bands are demanding!)

Moving on to talent, I claim that playing in a successful rock band requires at least as much natural talent as writing a computer game programming book. A band requires you to master a musical instrument. The book required Maneesh to learn how to program computer games. A band requires that you write original songs and develop your own style. The book required Maneesh to come up with a structure for presenting information about basic programming. A band requires that you're good enough at your instrument to play standard songs. The book required that Maneesh be a good enough writer that people wouldn't throw down the volume in disgust, but it certainly didn't require expert writing skill—it's a computer manual, not a literary novel. In short, the amount of talent required doesn't differ much between the two examples. No wellspring of hidden brilliance was tapped to make *Computer Game Programming for Teens* a reality.

To summarize, I tackled the standard arguments for what makes something impressive—hard work and talent—and established that playing in a rock band and writing a book are comparable. Yet writing a book blows away Stanford admissions officers in a way that playing in a rock band never would. If it's not hard work or talent, we can then ask, what is it that makes the book writing so impressive? Part 3 is an extended answer to this crucial question. In the chapters that follow, you'll learn about a powerful but little-understood phenomenon I call the *Failed-Simulation Effect*. This effect explains the paradox of the book versus the rock band and helps decode the success of almost every relaxed superstar I've encountered. In these chapters, you'll meet other students who, like Maneesh, leveraged this effect to get into their reach schools, even though their high school lives where uncluttered and relaxed. I'll highlight the general strategies they followed to integrate this effect into their student lives, and teach you how to do the same.

11

The Failed-Simulation Effect

MANEESH THE author blows us away. Maneesh the musician does not. This observation hints at an interesting phenomenon hidden outside the range of common understanding. In this chapter, I resolve the mystery by describing an overlooked but crucial admissions concept—a deceptively simple hypothesis that goes a long way toward explaining how relaxed superstars do what they do.

> **The Failed-Simulation-Effect Hypothesis**
> If you cannot mentally simulate the steps taken by a student to reach an accomplishment, you will experience a feeling of profound impressiveness.

Put another way, you are impressed by things that are hard to explain, regardless of whether or not they were hard to do. Consider the two different versions of Maneesh's story. Playing in a rock band doesn't generate the Failed-Simulation Effect. You can easily simulate the steps required for that accomplishment: buy an instrument, take lessons, practice, brood, and so on. There's no mystery. By contrast, publishing a bestselling book at the age of sixteen defies simulation. "How does a teenager get a book deal?" you ask in wonderment. This failure to simulate generates a sense of awed respect: "He must be something special."

Once you understand this effect, many of the seemingly random twists and turns of the admissions process suddenly make sense. It helps explain why students who you thought should get accepted had a hard time—even though they exhibited the traits you assumed were important—while other students surprised you by breezing into the Ivy League.

Consider the following two examples of real relaxed superstars who used this effect to succeed in admissions. (Later in Part 3, I'll detail exactly how they made these accomplishments happen.) The first student is named Kate. During her senior year of high school, Kate started an organization called the Varsity Study Team. It brought seniors from her private high school to work with seventh-graders in a well-known charter school servicing a rough neighborhood in Southeast Washington DC. As Kate describes it, she wanted to do more than "just help students with their homework." Instead, the organization focused on study and organization skills—"teaching the students how to outline their essay on Tuesday so they could do a better job writing on Wednesday." This program was deemed a success by the teachers at the charter school. Later that same year, Kate completed a research study of the reading techniques used by six of the best charter schools on the East Coast. The report was so well received that this same DC charter school adopted some of the findings in its classrooms. In short, Kate had a major impact on the lives of struggling students.

Kate's accomplishments clearly generate the Failed-Simulation Effect. You probably have no idea how a teenager can pull together an important study-skills program or wield original research to change the way a charter school teaches its pupils. The power of this effect was enough to get Kate into Princeton, even though, during her senior year, she took only four courses and participated in almost no extracurricular activities outside of her involvement with the charter school. With a hint of embarrassment, she admitted to me that she rarely had more than an hour or two of homework to finish during the average weekday—a small enough load that she often finished the work before she got home. The Failed-Simulation Effect, however, overwhelmed these factors.

For my next example, I want to return to Kara—the student described in the book's introduction. As you may recall, Kara developed a technology-based health curriculum that was adopted by school districts in ten different states. Once again, you probably have no idea how a high school student can have such a powerful effect on the country's educational system. Accordingly, you feel powerfully impressed—providing another clear example of the Failed-Simulation Effect in action.

Like Kate, Kara deserves the "relaxed" piece of the "relaxed superstar" title. Kara involved herself in few activities outside of her work on the curriculum, took a reasonable course load, and shockingly enough was happy to accept the occasional B to avoid late-night study marathons. The Failed-Simulation Effect was powerful enough, however, to swamp these concessions and help Kara get into twenty out of the whopping twenty-one schools to which she applied, including Stanford, Carnegie Mellon, Columbia, and MIT, where she now studies.

Maneesh, Kate, and Kara all wielded this effect to blow the socks off the admissions officers at their dream schools, even though they lived laid-back lives. They were impressive in a way that students who rely on basic traits like hard work and talent can't always replicate. Before moving on to detail exactly how these students got involved with their pursuits, I want to take a small detour to answer an important question: *Why does this effect exist?*

12

Lassiter's Insight

THE FAILED-SIMULATION EFFECT Hypothesis seems plausible. It dispels much of the mystery surrounding the admissions process—why, for example, we're so impressed by Maneesh, Kate, and Kara, but not by the equally hardworking students who devote their time to familiar pursuits like playing in a rock band or becoming class president. We are still left, however, with the question of why the Failed-Simulation Effect exists. That is, why is the inexplicable so impressive and the explicable so boring? To answer these questions, I turn your attention to the story of two competing research teams at Ohio University who, in the late 1990s, had the insight to turn a classic question of modern psychology on its head.

The Genius Effect

Over a period of several days in 1997, a group of seventy-eight undergraduates at Ohio University visited the lab of psychology professor Mark Alicke. They arrived, as scheduled, in pairs, having been told that they would participate in a study of intellectual skills. Each pair of students was led to a small classroom, where they sat side by side at desks. The walls were bare, except for a mirror. The students were given a test consisting of ten questions. The questions were visual puzzles, of the type found on IQ tests, and they required the test-takers to rotate and twist complicated shapes in their minds.

The puzzles were designed to be tricky; the average undergraduate at Ohio University could complete only three out of the ten. But in every session of this experiment, one of the two test-takers always did much better than this average, answering an outstanding seven out of ten questions correctly. He accomplished this feat because, as it turned out, the student was a confederate, hired by the researchers. He knew the answers in advance and was instructed to always score higher than the unwitting test-taker sitting beside him. To add insult to injury, this humiliation did not go unnoticed. Behind the mirror was a third student, who had arrived earlier and been instructed to quietly observe the entire process.

To understand the importance of this experiment, you have to step back to 1954, the year when a Stanford psychologist by the name of Leon Festinger proposed a simple idea, which was that our feelings about ourselves come from comparisons with other people. To the modern ear, this sounds obvious. But at the time, the impact was profound. Festinger's work kicked off half a century of inventive research that probed how different types of comparisons make us feel.

More than forty years later, Alicke's Ohio University experiment took Festinger's theory and flipped it. Alicke was not interested in how the unwitting test-taker felt about *himself* after the confederate scorched him on the test. He wanted to know instead how it made the test-taker feel about the *confederate*. It's a simple tweak, but given our interest in how people evaluate the impressiveness of others, it proves crucial to understanding the Failed-Simulation Effect.

After the tests were completed and scored, the fooled test-taker, whom I'll call *the subject*, was asked to rate both his and the confederate's intelligence on a ten-point scale. The subject, of course, didn't know that his partner was a plant, so he wasn't feeling too hot about himself, having just been trounced. Not surprisingly, the subjects rated themselves, on average, 4.28, while rating the confederate a much higher 7.51.

The real insight, however, came from the third student, who watched from behind the mirror. When this student, whom I'll call *the observer*, was also asked to rate the intelligence of the two test-takers, he rated the subjects, on average, 4.33, which basically matched the score of 4.28 that the subjects gave themselves. But when the observer rated the confederates, he gave them an average score 6.44—a full point lower than the average score of 7.51 given to them by the defeated subjects. In other words, the subject, who'd just been beaten badly on the test, thought the confederate was a really smart guy. The observer, watching the same test disinterestedly through the mirror, was less impressed.

Alicke and his collaborators dubbed this result the Genius Effect, as in, "The only way I'm comfortable with someone beating me is if he's a genius." They hypothesized that we inflate the ability of people who outperform us so that we can heal our fragile egos. To use the analogy given by Alicke in the original paper, the tennis pro at your local club won't be upset if he's trounced in a match against Andy Roddick. In the context of Alicke's experiment, if the subject assumes that the confederate is the Andy Roddick of intelligence tests, then he won't sweat being beaten. It's in the subject's best interest to assume that the confederate's a really talented guy.

But was Alicke right?

Several years later, a different team at Ohio University, led by professor Daniel Lassiter, challenged Alicke's hypothesis. Lassiter began by re-creating the 1997 experiment and found the same results: the subject consistently inflated the confederate's smarts. But Lassiter then introduced a twist. He hypothesized that the Genius Effect was not about ego. He claimed that it instead revealed a much simpler truth, which is that when judging people we use ourselves as a convenient point of comparison. When it comes to things like intelligence tests, people think they are much smarter than they actually are, so when they do poorly they assume the other guy must be really smart. It's not about repairing one's ego, it's instead a snap judgment based on imperfect assumptions.

To test this idea, Lassiter conducted a survey of Ohio University undergrads. He found, as expected, that most of these students assumed that they would be good at intelligence tests. In fact, the majority predicted that they would score better than another student in a head-to-head competition. Like Lake Wobegon, Ohio University is a place where everyone thinks he or she is above average.

Now reconsider Alicke's experiment in light of this new hypothesis. A subject and a confederate sit down in an isolated room to take a test. According to Lassiter's survey, the subject probably thinks he's pretty good at these tests. Then the subject does poorly. If Lassiter is right, and the subject uses himself as a convenient benchmark for evaluating the confederate, he will conclude: "If I'm good at these tests and this guy did better than I did, he must be *really* good." He then assigns the confederate a high intelligence score. This is not ego, just a quick decision based on a self-comparison.

And now consider the observer. Though he too may feel strongly about his own test-taking skills, he has no reason to think that the subject is anything special. When the subject gets beaten, therefore, the observer is not as impressed by the confederate and therefore doesn't score him as high. In other words, the subject thinks of the confederate as someone who defeated an above-average test-taker, while the observer thinks of the confederate as defeating only an average test-taker.

Both Alicke's ego theory and Lassiter's comparison idea are plausible explanations for the Genius Effect observed in these experiments. But who was right?

This is where Lassiter's twist comes in. The professor cleverly altered the experiment as follows. In 50 percent of the trials, chosen at random, the research assistant running the experiment casually mentions to the observer that he's heard that the subject is really good at these tests. In other words, the researcher tries to get the observer to think as highly of the subject as the subject does of himself. If Lassiter is right, then this priming should make the subject's and the observer's impressions of the confederate converge. If Lassiter is wrong, and repairing ego is the key factor, then the subject should continue to rate the confederate higher, because he feels bad about losing and in his quest to repair his ego he will push the confederate's intelligence score as high as possible. The observer, with no ego damage to repair, will not go as far with his scores.

After the experiment was conducted, and the numbers crunched, it turned out that in the cases where the extra information was given, the scores of the subject and the observer became statistically identical. Lassiter was right: forget ego, to judge other people we use ourselves as a convenient benchmark. The Genius Effect observed in the test-taking environment was the combination of this simple truth with the fact that students tend to think they're good at tests of this kind. As I'll argue next, the reach of the Genius Effect extends beyond the psychology lab of Ohio University and into the world of college admissions decisions.

From the Genius Effect to Extracurricular Activities

Imagine two hypothetical students whom I'll call Mia and Jon. Mia is the first-chair violinist in her school orchestra and Jon drives into the city once a week to take Japanese calligraphy lessons. Mia and Jon are following standard admissions orthodoxy by focusing on activities that demonstrate traits such as hard work, some talent, and, in the case of Jon, unusualness. According to the Failed-Simulation Effect, however, neither of their activities will generate a feeling of impressiveness because they're not inexplicable. (You can probably simulate exactly what is required for both of their accomplishments: practicing in the case of Mia and attending a weekly lesson in the case of Jon.)

Lassiter's research helps us understand this reaction. When evaluating the impressiveness of Mia, for example, we learned from the Ohio University studies that you're using yourself as a convenient point of comparison. You probably learned how to play an instrument at some point in your life, or at least know someone who did. Because of this, you know what it takes to become really good at the violin: practicing hard. You agree, therefore, that Mia is a hard worker. If you were rating her diligence, then your self-comparison would lead to a high score because you likely imagine yourself to be a hard worker and she did a lot more hard work than you. But you're not rating her diligence, you're instead considering her *impressiveness*, which most people tend to think of as a measure of intrinsic ability. (In American culture, as I argued in the Part 2 playbook, we're much more impressed with people who have some magical ability than with those who simply work hard. That is, we love Michael Jordan and Matt Damon's character from *Good Will Hunting*, but we are indifferent to the valedictorian who studies ten hours a day.)

When you compare Mia to yourself, therefore, you don't see a special intrinsic ability that you lack. She coupled hard practice with perhaps a dollop of musical talent, but you too could become pretty good at the violin if you practiced as hard. So when it comes to rating her natural abilities, your self-comparison generates a mediocre review. On the other hand, if she had gotten so far with the violin that it defied your ability to simulate—say she played at Carnegie Hall—the Failed-Simulation Effect would return, as the path to this level of accomplishment is beyond what you could imagine yourself traveling.

The argument against Jon's seeming impressive is equally clear. You probably have no doubt that you too could learn Japanese calligraphy if you wanted to. Go to Google. Search for nearby instructors. Sign up for a class. *Done*. When you compare Jon to yourself, you once again find no intrinsic ability that you lack.

Now let's return to Maneesh, from the opening chapter of Part 3. Here things get interesting. Think for a moment about how your self-comparison unfolds in relation to this student. You probably ran into trouble because, unlike what Mia and Jon did, what Maneesh did defies explanation. You cannot compare Maneesh's ability to publish books to your own ability, because you have no idea what this goal requires. Whereas for Jon and Mia you could quickly simulate yourself repeating their efforts (with enough extra effort), and therefore not grant them much credit for special skills. Maneesh forces you to confront an unsettling scenario: he accomplished something that you couldn't—no matter how much effort you imagine yourself investing. Like the subject who's outscored by a confederate taking the same intelligence test, you cannot escape the asymmetry of the scenario. Maneesh has done something you *couldn't* do, so he must possess something special. As a result, you're impressed.

I can reduce these ideas into three simple insights:

* Research shows that you evaluate other people by first comparing them to yourself.

* If during this comparison you can't imagine yourself doing
  what someone else did, then you're left to assume that he
  or she possesses some ability that you lack.
* In American culture, impressiveness is tied more to special
  abilities than it is to persistence or inventiveness.

These insights combine to an inescapable conclusion: the Failed-Simulation Effect makes perfect sense—we are most impressed by activities that are hard to explain.

I hope I've convinced you that the Failed-Simulation Effect is fundamental to the way your mind works. This is a powerful observation; the effect allows you to separate impressiveness from backbreaking work and the stress such efforts bring. In other words, it's a key ingredient in the relaxed superstar stew.

With this crucial concept in hand, you're left with the task of figuring out how to introduce this effect into your own extracurricular life. I address this challenge in the chapters that follow.

13

The Three Rules of Innovation

FOR CONVENIENCE, I'll use the word "innovative" to describe activities that generate the Failed-Simulation Effect. I like this word because it's not commonly used in the context of college admissions and I'm trying to emphasize the difference between the type of pursuits that produce this effect and the type that most students *think* are important. The former tend to be engaging and manageable while the latter are time-consuming and stressful.

I first introduced the idea of innovative activities in a blog post during the summer of 2008. The idea was an immediate hit—many of my readers said that the concept helped them make sense of the admissions process.

But there was a problem.

An understanding of the Failed-Simulation Effect doesn't necessarily help students deploy this force in their own lives. Consider the following comments I received on my 2008 post:

❋ "The Failed-Simulation Effect really helped explain things. But I'm still trying to find my own mind-blowing activity."

* "Awesome post . . . but how can I apply it as a research-oriented student? I guess I should volunteer to be an RA, do independent research, etc., but how do I push this to the 'wow' level?"

* "I'm trying to figure out what activity to take part in next year, and though this article helped I'm still relatively clueless."

* "[I'm having] a hard time coming up with that original idea. How do I find an innovative experience in my field of interest?"

These comments, which are just a few from among many similar ones, demonstrate a common reaction to the idea of activity innovation. At first the student is elated to discover that there's a rational explanation for why some accomplishments are more impressive than others. But then the student sits back and asks himself or herself: "Okay, what innovative activity can I do?" As ideas fail to form, the elation fades.

In this chapter, I want to help you avoid such a fate. Below, I define what I call *the three rules of innovation*—three pieces of advice you should heed if you want innovation to become a feature of your extracurricular life. In the next chapter, I'll help cement your understanding of these concepts by returning to the stories of Maneesh, Kate, and Kara and identifying exactly where the three rules aided their transformation from average to innovative.

Rule 1: Innovators Don't Try to Think Up Innovations from Scratch
The students who commented on my blog post got stuck because they disobeyed this rule. It's nearly impossible to think up an innovative activity from scratch—so don't try. Maneesh and Kate and Kara didn't have brilliant brainstorms that led them directly to their innovative activities. The paths they followed were long and circuitous.

Obeying this rule is difficult because it requires patience. Your instinct is to want to find something *right now* that can help you stand out. The idea that you might have to wait until some unforeseeable future moment is scary. "What if it never comes?" you ask yourself with understandable trepidation. I hope the following two rules, combined with the stories in the next chapter, will provide the courage you need to trust that this patience will translate into rewards.

Its difficulties aside, it shouldn't surprise you that rule 1 is true. Recall the definition of the Failed-Simulation Effect, which requires that the average person cannot mentally simulate the steps someone took to produce an accomplishment. If you could think up an innovative pursuit from scratch, it follows that you could mentally simulate the steps required to achieve it—otherwise you wouldn't have considered it a possibility. This implies that other people could do the same; so the pursuit, by definition, cannot generate the effect. It's an admissions catch-22.

Groucho Marx famously said, "I don't care to belong to any club that will accept me as a member." You should apply this logic, with a slight tweak, in your admissions journey: you shouldn't care to be involved with any activity that you can easily imagine being involved with. The real path to innovation is often much longer, and it generally has many more intermediate steps. But the length and complexity are what separates accomplishments that are innovative from those that can easily be imagined. Fear not, however. In the two rules that follow, I'll provide you with the guidance necessary to navigate this route.

Rule 2: Innovators Join Closed Communities and Pay Their Dues

In the world of extracurricular activities there are three types of communities: *open*, *hidden*, and *closed*. Understanding these distinctions is crucial for fostering innovation.

An *open* community is one that most people know about and understand. School government, for example, is open; you probably know all about becoming class president or class secretary. There is little mystery about how this world operates: getting elected requires putting up posters, giving speeches, and mixing an aura of responsibility with a dash of popularity. You know that class officers hold weekly meetings, plan dances, and can usually effect only small-scale changes in the school—perhaps changing the vending machine contents or negotiating for new parking spaces. People may respect your hard work if you succeed in this world, but the process is so well understood that it's unlikely to generate the Failed-Simulation Effect.

Hidden communities are those that are completely unknown to most people. For example, if I told you that I was a second-level game master in a countywide LARP league, this would (hopefully) mean very little to you. LARP, as I discovered from watching the 2008 movie *Role Models*, and certainly not from personal experience, stands for Live-Action Role Playing. From what I understand, it involves people dressing up like wizards and monsters and fighting in local parks using padded swords. Most normal people have never heard of this community and understand nothing about how it works. It might have required a virtuosic talent to become a second-level game master, and in the LARP world this rank might be considered a very difficult and rare accomplishment—right up there with talking to a girl—but because the community is hidden, the outside world doesn't recognize the value of this accomplishment. The fact that other people can't simulate the steps I took to earn the rank is not enough to generate the Failed-Simulation Effect because the outside observer doesn't understand what it is that I accomplished in the first place.

Then there are communities of the third type: those that are *closed*. This is the sweet spot for innovation. A closed community is one that most people know about but whose operations

they don't understand. Each of our relaxed superstar examples
in Part 3 worked within a closed community. Maneesh wrote a
book. Everyone knows what it means to be an author, but few
know the details of how book deals are done. Kate changed the
way a charter school taught reading. Everyone went to school
and knows about classroom curricula, but few know the details
of how these curricula are evaluated and changed. A similar
argument holds for Kara and her health curriculum. Everyone
remembers health class, but few know what it takes to change
what a school teaches in this class. The combination of familiar-
ity and mystery that defines a closed community is what makes it
a perfect breeding ground for innovation.

Once you've identified a closed community, your next step is
to gain access. If you walked in the front door of a charter school
and, inspired by Kate, declared that you want to do research to
help them improve the way they teach their students, the harried teachers would barely take the time to stifle a laugh before
escorting you back out onto the street. To take action in such a
community you must instead first prove that you belong. There's
no shortcut here; you have to pay your dues. As you'll learn in
the next chapter, all three of our innovative students paid some
serious dues before they gained access to innovative opportunities within their communities.

Students don't always like to hear this message. Many tell me
that they're impatient to start something right away that's going
to help them shine. I'm always somewhat sad to have to clue
them in to the reality of dues-paying, but it's an immutable law.
I would go so far as to counsel you to not even waste your time
thinking about potential innovative activities until after your
dues-paying is well under way. This will prevent you from trying
to do too much, too fast, which can spoil the trust you want to
establish before it fully forms. There's also a hidden benefit to
dues-paying. During this process you'll begin to develop a more

sophisticated understanding of how the relevant field operates—an understanding that will prove essential later when you try to develop a project that's both impressive and feasible.

Rule 3: Innovators Leverage Their Way up to Innovation

Here's the scene: You've found a closed community and talked your way into an entry-level position. For the past few months you've being paying your dues by cheerfully and quickly accomplishing *everything* the members have pushed in your direction. You've also shown genuine interest and asked lots of questions. It seems as if they're finally starting to trust you. Because you've been working in this closed community for a while, you're beginning to unravel the mystery of how it operates. Once you understand the mechanics, you begin to notice opportunities for projects that would probably seem innovative to the outside world. What do you do next?

Your instinct might be to propose the biggest, boldest, most innovative project possible. I don't recommend that strategy—it rarely works. Even if the members of the community trust and like you, they probably don't trust you *enough* to give you free reign on something big and important. When you hear the stories of Maneesh, Kate, and Kara in the next chapter, you'll notice that they ramped up their innovation through a series of increasingly ambitious projects before finally arriving at the big accomplishments that earned them the bulk of their recognition. Instead of asking, "What's the *most* innovative project I could propose?" they asked, "What's a project that I'm well suited to finish efficiently and competently right now?" Each such completion made even bigger, more innovative projects available. By leveraging one project to get to the next—each one appropriate for their current level of experience—they ended up somewhere amazing.

Once again, patience locates itself in the center of your

admissions endeavor. Innovators leverage one project to get to the next, moving from small and reasonable to large and innovative. They don't try to leap into the deep end right at the beginning. This strategy is longer, to be sure, but the end results are better and more assured.

Living the Three Rules

Hopefully, the three rules of innovation will help you sidestep the frustration that often accompanies an understanding of the Failed-Simulation Effect. If you abandon the misguided idea that you can think up something innovative *right now*, and instead enter a closed community, pay your dues, and leverage your way up to larger projects, massively impressive innovation can become a part of your student life. The key point here—the point that throws so many students off the innovation scent—is that you cannot predict your ultimate destination until you're well along the path. My goal for the remainder of Part 3 is to give you enough confidence to soldier through this uncertainty to your eventual innovation-fueled glory.

14

A Tale of Three Innovations

YOU'VE HEARD the theory; now it's time see some real-world examples. Below, I tell the stories of how Maneesh, Kate, and Kara got started down their roads to innovation. As I proceed, I'll highlight the places where the three rules of innovation played their starring role.

How Maneesh Got a Book Deal

When I first spoke with Maneesh, in the late fall of 2008, he struggled to answer a simple question: "What makes you different?" After some false starts, he paused for a second and then said: "I want to tell you a story."

A few days before our conversation, Maneesh had been walking through a park when he came across a group of bartenders doing tricks. They were throwing bottles in the air, juggling them, and catching them behind their backs. A crowd had formed. "People where in awe," he recalls. "They were thinking, 'How do they do that?'"

Maneesh walked up to the bartenders and asked if they taught a class. ("I thought it would be really cool to learn.")

"Dude," one of the bartenders answered, laughing, "we've been doing this for only three or four days; it's not that hard."

Impressed, Maneesh spent the next half hour learning some basic moves. Soon he too was juggling bottles.

"The people around me were really in awe," he said.

Maneesh's entrance into the publishing world has much in common with that day in the park; it was a bold move prompted by an indifference to conventional wisdom. His story begins a decade earlier, when a young Maneesh, infected by the tech enthusiasm sweeping the West Coast during the dot-com boom of the late 1990s, became obsessed with computer game programming. Like many young proto-nerds of the era, he devoured technical manuals and learned how to design rudimentary games. He even started a company with his friends, awarding it the solemn title Cold Vector Games. He now admits: "We made a few games, but never sold anything."

At this early stage, we see the first two rules of innovation in action. Maneesh didn't start with the idea of publishing a book. Instead, he entered the closed community of computer game programming and began paying his dues with long afternoons in front of the monitor.

At the age of twelve, Maneesh convinced his parents to take him to a computer programming conference held in nearby Santa Clara, California. He recalls: "My hero at the time, an editor of computer programming titles, was there, and I got to meet him and find out more about his publishing house." Motivated by the encounter, Maneesh went home and began to explore the publishing company's Web site. In one of the company's forums he encountered a post by the editor that listed some book ideas in need of authors. One of the ideas was a computer game programming guide for teenagers.

A wave of inspiration washed over Maneesh. He sent an e-mail to the editor, whom he had just met earlier that day, and pitched the idea that the best person to write a book for teenagers was an actual teenager.

"I will never ever let anyone under the age of twenty-five write a book for me," the editor replied. Crushed, Maneesh abandoned the idea.

The next year, however, Maneesh returned to the same conference. While wandering the convention hall, he stumbled into a young kid messing around with a piece of software called Blitz Basic. This was a computer game programming language that Maneesh had mastered, and it was the same language that he had imagined featuring in his computer game programming book. A new boldness formed. "I could make this book work," he thought.

Returning home, he wrote forty pages of sample material, comprising the first three chapters of the proposed book. He e-mailed the chapters to the editor, telling him, in essence, "I know you said no, but check this out first."

A few days later, the editor replied. "This is actually good," he said.

The editor passed the pages on to other executives at the publishing house, and they eventually agreed to the idea of a teenager writing a book for teenagers. Advances for technical guides are relatively small, so there wasn't much to lose.

It took Maneesh a long time to write all thirteen chapters. "I wrote it over a couple of years, spending about two hours per week," he recalls. "In the end, I was a year and three months overdue."

When the book was finally published, it was a minor hit among teenagers who, like Maneesh, wanted a quick guide to programming simple recreational games. His theory had been vindicated—it took a teenager to produce material that could connect with fickle-minded fellow teenagers, whose attention span was short. After a while, some librarians, noticing the influx of kids asking for the title, invited Maneesh to speak at their local branches. Somewhere in this period, a producer from the newly launched cable channel TechTV heard one of Maneesh's speeches and asked the young author to appear on a Q&A segment for one of the channel's new experimental shows. The show was soon scrapped, but Maneesh's appearances were enough to push his book (briefly) up to number 16 in amazon .com's sales rankings. This made it, in a loose sense of the word, a *bestseller*—a moniker that would play a big role in Maneesh's college applications.

In this transition from initial idea to bestseller, the third rule of innovation comes into play. For his first projects within the closed community of computer game programming, Maneesh developed increasingly complicated games. He leveraged this activity into a project to write sample chapters to pitch to an editor who was looking for a related book. Only once this project had succeeded did he start writing the full book itself—the eventual source of impressiveness that helped this laid-back star get into Stanford.

Maneesh's path to innovation spanned a relatively long period of time. Years were devoted to mastering computer game programming, and only once this skill was in place did he unleash the rapid series of leverages that led to the book. By contrast, Kate's story of becoming a charter school reformer, which I'll tell next, is contained within a single year. It demonstrates how, with the right strategy, innovation can happen fast.

How Kate Made a Difference

"My high school class was extraordinarily impressive," Kate told me. "We had the highest SAT scores in the school's history, we all took hard courses, and we all studied really hard. The teachers called us 'the good class.'"

It is not surprising, then, that during her junior year of high school, Kate fell into a cycle of overwork. She was the editor of the school newspaper, a serious member of the government club, and like thousands of admissions-focused students who came before her, she volunteered at a free medical clinic. In addition, she played tennis and lacrosse, and was on the youth council of her church. She sat for six AP tests that year, and because of this she spent at least three to six hours on homework every night. This load took its toll.

"I was totally sleep-deprived. This made me into a total brat. It was really stressful," she recalls.

Then everything changed.

During her senior year, Kate dropped down to only four courses. Two of them were APs; the others she describes as "really, really easy and low key." She resigned as editor of the paper, reduced her government club responsibilities, and gave up her time-consuming position on the church's youth council. She stopped volunteering at the medical clinic and left the lacrosse team. With this simplification complete, her life became bearable once again.

Looking back on that year, Kate describes the time as "fun and less stressful." She started going to bed at 9:30 most nights, and she estimates that there were only three or four occasions where she got less than eight hours of sleep.

"It was great," she recalls. "I would get up early, make breakfast for my family. I had time to do things on weekends instead of outlining my entire U.S. history textbook."

Yet even after all of these simplifications, Kate was accepted at Princeton. In fact, as she would argue, it was *because* of these simplifications that she got in. The reason she drastically reduced her schedule was to focus her attention on a single project:

working at a nearby charter school. By the end of that year she had set up an effective tutoring program and conducted research that changed the way the school taught reading to its students. These accomplishments were clearly innovative, and the resulting Failed-Simulation Effect got her into Princeton (while her harder-working, higher-scoring friends had to settle for the waitlist). What's important for our purposes here, however, is to understand exactly how Kate made this drastic transformation from a grind to an innovator.

To better explain Kate's story, I'll use the three rules of innovation as a guide. Rule 1 says that innovators don't think up their innovations from scratch. This was true for Kate. Charter schools tend to be insular, and the school where Kate would eventually work was part of a network that has a reputation for being especially suspicious of outsiders (she was worried enough about this to ask that I avoid identifying the school by name). There was no way that she could have come up with her innovative projects from scratch—the school staff would have had no patience with a kid they didn't know claiming to have a big idea.

Instead, Kate's start was humble. During her junior year, she volunteered to be a teacher's aide for one of the fifth-grade teachers at her own elite DC-area private school. Her motivations were simple: teaching interested her, and her dad, who'd attended the same school as a child, had had the same volunteer gig and suggested that she try it. Big innovative projects were not on her mind at this early stage.

"It's hard as a high school student to just sit around and think up some fascinating thing—like some entirely new organization or magazine," she confirmed. "It's much easier to just find something you're really interested in and show them that you could be useful."

During this year, Kate's responsibilities were standard. She would make photocopies or help the students prepare for a lesson. At first she would answer the stray grammar question when the teacher was otherwise occupied. "I might walk over and help if a student was like, 'I don't know what a noun is,'" Kate recalled. Eventually, the teacher allowed Kate's responsibilities to grow. By the end of the semester, Kate was teaching a grammar lesson three times a week, on her own, to a group of students.

Rule 2 says that innovators enter a closed community and pay their dues. This matches Kate's path. She entered the community of teaching and made herself as useful as possible. Eventually the teacher began to see her as indispensable, and this is where Kate landed her first break. It started when her teacher got a new job at a charter school that had just opened across town.

"What am I going to do without you next year?" the teacher asked.

"What am I going to do without my time in the fifth-grade classroom?" Kate replied. She had grown fond of her students—an important source of stress relief in the middle of her hectic junior year schedule. The pair hatched a plan: they would try to convince the school to let Kate spend time as a teaching assistant at the charter school. The teacher helped Kate put together a reading list and devise a series of writing assignments that she would complete in an effort to give the proposal enough academic heft to qualify as an independent study project.

"There were tons of roadblocks," Kate admits, but she and her teacher-mentor finally got the administrators to agree to a plan that had Kate leave school each day at 11 a.m., travel across town to the charter school, and spend an hour and a half in the classroom, observing and helping. As part of the independent study project, she was supposed to then return home and spend the rest of the normal school-day hours reading about educational reform and writing essays on what she was learning. This hybrid schedule was what motivated Kate to drastically reduce her commitments during her senior year. She wanted to do this one project very well, and she worried that running back and forth between her charter schoolwork and a dozen unrelated activities would sap her concentration.

Kate quickly earned her keep at the new school. "At first, I would come in and observe for an hour and a half and then leave," she remembers. But as time went on and she got to know the staff better, she began to hang around longer and make herself more useful. "I started to get more responsibility and eventually they were treating me like I was part of their faculty."

Rule 3 says that after you pay your dues, you should leverage your way from small projects into larger projects. Kate followed this rule by leveraging her position as a fifth-grade teacher's aide into a position as an observer at a charter school. Once there, she returned to rule 2 and once again began paying her dues. Only after spending an entire semester working hard at the charter school did she return to rule 3 and leverage herself up to something bigger.

At the end of her first semester at the charter school, Kate proposed a tutoring program called Varsity Study Teams. "I didn't want to just do homework help," she explains. Instead, she identified the thirty most struggling seventh-grade students at the school and then brought in seniors from her private school to work with them on their study and organization skills. "I couldn't have done this if I hadn't gotten to know the faculty at the charter school," Kate says. Their trust translated into permission to begin the project on a trial basis. Because her schedule was otherwise empty, Kate had more than enough time to make sure that the program was a success.

During this same period she had to decide on a culminating project for her independent study. Over the past few months, she had learned a lot about the operation of charter schools and their underlying philosophies. She had also earned the respect of the teachers at the charter school. These factors made serious research possible. She proposed that she study the reading programs at six high-performing charter schools on the East Coast. Her friends at her DC charter school helped arrange for her to observe classrooms and interview teachers at each of the schools. These interviews would have been impossible to set up without the strong support of her own school—yet another argument for dues-paying.

As Kate traveled the East Coast, she spent a day at a school in the Bronx that had, incredibly, 100 percent of its students reading at grade level. "To have a hundred percent reading proficiency was just astronomical," Kate says.

At the time, the accepted wisdom among charter schools was that reading instruction should be strategy-based and take place communally. At Kate's school, for example, the teacher would introduce a new reading strategy and then walk the kids through applying the strategy together on the same chapters of the same book. The teachers at this school in the Bronx, however, did things differently. As Kate soon discovered, their approach was to get the kids to read as many books as possible each year.

"By the time an upper-middle-class student reaches the fifth grade, they've read something like three hundred books total, ranging from picture books to young adult chapter books," Kate noted. With this in mind, the teachers at the school in the Bronx focused relentlessly on closing the gap between those students and their own fifth-graders, most of whom were from less-privileged backgrounds. To accomplish this, they would first introduce the same reading strategies used by most charter schools. But after only eight or nine minutes of discussing a given strategy, they would dedicate the remainder of the class period to helping the students read whatever they wanted.

"I walked into the classroom, and there were thirty little

heads bent over whatever book they liked—the new Harry Potter or something from the Diary of a Wimpy Kid series—all of them practicing the strategy of the day as they read," Kate recalls. "For an entire hour, the teacher would walk around and ask each student individually what's going on in their book." This was a radical departure from the standard model, in which all the students were kept together.

Kate pulled together her research into a paper that she presented to the teachers at her charter school. They immediately grasped the implications. "It changed how they taught," Kate said. "My mentor, for example, now starts every class with thirty minutes of independent reading."

Kate's story provides a textbook example of the rules of innovation in action. Instead of trying to think up something fantastic from scratch, she joined a closed community, paid her dues, and then kept leveraging her projects. She started by making photocopies in a fifth-grade classroom at her private school, but ended up, less than a year later, conducting important research for one of the country's most successful charter school networks.

By the time she sat down for a Princeton admissions interview, the power of her innovations-in-progress became clear. "My interviews were all about my work at the charter school," she recalls. "They loved that I dropped my extracurriculars and took only four classes. They said: 'We see so many students who are in model UN and the debate club, but who know nothing about the real world.'" Kate's subsequent acceptance at Princeton came as no surprise.

In the last of these stories, told below, you'll encounter another student who used systematic dues-paying and leveraging to leap up the ranks of an organization and into the realm where innovation is common.

Kara Gets Healthy

When you first met Kara, in the introduction to this book, you learned that the classmates at her competitive high school were surprised when she got accepted into most of her reach schools, including Columbia, MIT, and Stanford. Kara had ignored the culture of overwork that dominated her high school. Instead, she maintained a reasonable course load and didn't sweat the occasional B—the habit that caused her college counselor endless consternation.

Her admissions success was instead generated by innovation—specifically, the work Kara did for a San Jose–based, high-tech community service center dubbed the Digital Clubhouse. By the time she was filling out her college applications, she could report that she had single-handedly developed and tested a health curriculum—focused on avoiding diabetes through healthy eating—that was adopted by school districts in ten different states. When you hear this accomplishment described for the first time, it's hard to avoid the Failed-Simulation Effect. You're probably clueless as to how a teenager could make such a difference all by herself. The result is a wave of impressiveness—the same factor that helped Kara get accepted almost everywhere she applied. What's striking about Kara's story, however, is that her ascent to awe-inspiring innovation was so natural and painless that it took her a while to realize the importance of her endeavor.

"It didn't hit me until near the end of the project that this was a big deal," she told me. "I was thinking about it step by step, saying, 'I just need to get through these next three hours.'"

Like Maneesh and Kate, Kara never experienced a flash-of-genius insight. At no point did she yell "Aha!" and then commit herself to launching a massive new health curriculum. Instead, she followed the three rules of innovation, which led her to true impressiveness.

Kara's story starts with two friends, Alex and Greg. The three students helped convince the school to start up a FIRST robotics club, an experience that drew them closer. Kara, however, became annoyed that Alex and Greg were never available to work on Saturdays. She soon discovered that they were volunteering at a local community center called the Digital Clubhouse. "You should really come along," Greg pressed, fed up with Kara's annoyance. She relented.

When Kara first arrived, she discovered that her two friends were helping with a project to videotape testimonials from the area's aging population of World War II veterans—an effort sponsored by the Smithsonian Institution. She had joined a closed community. Now, in the spirit of rules 1 and 2, it was time to pay her dues.

The project required five hours a week. Three of those hours were dedicated to interviewing. Every Saturday, each team was given a camera and the address of a veteran to interview (close to fifty student volunteers were involved with the project). They were then expected to find two hours later in the week to edit the interview into the appropriate length and format.

"When I first started volunteering for the project, I would tag along with more experienced members and receive training," Kara recalls. "After a while I worked up to filming my own interviews and training new people."

After investing the effort to learn filming and editing skills, Kara was ready for her break when it came along during her sophomore year. She arrived one Saturday morning at a veteran's house. At this point, the interview process had become routine. In her head, as the taping progressed, she could imagine the exact points where she would later make the editing cuts. But this morning, it took only a few minutes to realize that she had stumbled into something special. The veteran, an African-

American man who had served as a Navy chef because he had been barred from fighting, was a natural storyteller.

"His story was dramatic, and he had this deep, raspy voice that just kept you interested," Kara recalls. "I was good enough at editing at this point to take what I had and make the most of it."

The higher-ups at the Digital Clubhouse agreed. They selected the interview to showcase at a fund-raising dinner. The mix of a powerful storyteller and a compelling narrative made the clip a perfect fit for the event. "I was lucky," Kara notes. So was the Digital Clubhouse—the video helped raise a lot of money.

As a reward for the interview's success, the head of the organization asked Kara if there were any particular projects she wanted to work on. This is where rule 3 enters the scene. Kara was faced with the opportunity to leverage her good work within a closed community into a larger project. She wouldn't let the opportunity pass.

"At the time I was aware of the diabetes epidemic that was sweeping the area where we lived," Kara recalls. "There had been this big movement at my school, for example, to remove the soda machines because we were seeing all of these new cases in our neighborhood. So I mentioned the idea of working on the issue."

"Oh, yeah, that's been on the news a lot recently," the head of the organization replied. "That's a good idea; maybe you can work on that."

Kara had heard about another project at the organization— the use of a computer-based curriculum to take antidrug education into local schools. It hadn't been terribly successful, and its future was uncertain. She proposed that she could revamp the curriculum—changing the focus from drugs to healthy eating. "This idea was well received," she recalls. "They told me to think about how to craft the project and then come back with a more developed idea."

This step validates the importance of getting to know a closed community before looking for innovation opportunities. Having spent a year working with the Digital Clubhouse, Kara had enough insider knowledge to build a targeted proposal with a very good chance of acceptance. Investigating changes to an existing program was far more palatable to the organization than investing resources in something brand new.

Kara's research on the topic started with the Internet, progressed to books, and then eventually to interviews with doctors. She used the information she'd gleaned to build a proposal for a class consisting of modules. Each module was centered on using the computer to complete a project related to diabetes prevention. For example, one of the modules had the students design a poster about healthy eating habits. (A key piece of the Digital Clubhouse's mission is to integrate the learning of computer skills with unrelated educational goals.)

"I talked to a lot of people in the organization during this time," Kara recalls. "Every two weeks or so, somebody would ask, 'Have you done anything?' and I would show them what I was up to." Fortunately, Kara enjoyed the work. Because it was self-directed and free of hard deadlines, it became something she wanted to do—a true deep interest. "It was the work I would do when I was bored with homework and wanted to procrastinate," she said. In the end, it took around eight months to complete the proposal.

Eight months.

This point is important enough to merit a brief aside. At this stage in your student career, you've probably never faced a project that couldn't be completed in a couple days of hard work. To adopt a mind-set conducive to innovation, however, you need to recalibrate your understanding of effort. Forget a few days of hard work. Quality results often require, as Kara discovered, *months* of effort. The key here is that work spread over such a long time doesn't have to be overwhelming. Kara, for example, didn't work late into the night for eight months straight. Instead, she did the work a little at a time, in reasonable bursts. When considering your own dues-paying, keep this in mind. Doing a reasonable amount of hard work each day, over a long period of time, produces better results than doing a lot of hard work in a short period of time. Mastering this approach will separate you from the vast majority of your peers who lack such patience.

After eight months of consistent work, Kara had devised a detailed plan that captured exactly what would be taught at each moment of each course—with copious research to support its lessons.

"I was able to say, 'Look, I have a specific course plan and timeline for this and I know what materials I need and how many people it will require, and I have a lesson plan,'" she said. The extra effort paid off. The organization approved the next step: sending Kara to shadow real teachers and use the information to polish the plan further.

Kara had discovered a common theme of youth accomplishment: If you surpass people's expectations on small projects, they will reward you with a shot at something big and interesting. After a period of observing teachers in the classroom, and using the experience to polish her lesson plan even more, Kara finally got her chance to test her curriculum in front of real students. She was assigned an elementary school in a rundown San Jose neighborhood, and was given one afternoon each week to teach her class as part of an after-school program.

"I remember thinking at some point that all of my hard work had come down to making a group of seven-year-olds like me," she recalls. Fortunately, over the ten-week span of the class, things proceeded smoothly. "The challenge of teaching a three-hour class is to avoid having the kids think, 'Oh my God, I've been here for three hours!'" Kara said. She had learned from her shadowing experience, however, how to insert huge shifts within each class to break it up and make it go faster. "You have to make it feel like things are always moving."

By the end of the experience, the curriculum had undergone major changes—most built around the reality of seven-year-old attention spans. The program was deemed solid, and Digital Clubhouse distributed the curriculum to the other schools in the district that were already using the organization's antidrug program. From here, growth accelerated. After the various schools in the district reported that it had gone well, the organization passed on the curriculum to its partner centers in ten different states. These centers, in turn, distributed it to the local school districts that they already worked with. At this point, Kara could claim that she had custom-designed a curriculum used across the country.

Like those of Kate and Maneesh, Kara's path was smoothed by the cycle of dues-paying and leveraging prescribed by the three rules of innovation. It took close to two years of effort from first joining the community to blowing the socks off admissions officers, but the end effect was much more impressive—and much less stressful—than the overload strategy followed by her peers.

Pulling the Stories Together

All three of these stories emphasize the power of the three rules of innovation. Their message is clear: Stop seeking a flash of insight that will make you stunningly impressive all at once. Instead, get your foot in the door in the right type of community, do good work, and then once you understand the community and have earned its trust, begin to leverage. The utility of this approach is obscured by its simplicity, but don't be fooled—it works.

In the playbook that follows, I'll provide specific advice for making these three rules a practical part of your own life. The goal is to simplify your transition into a student like Maneesh, Kate, and Kara, who traded overloaded schedules and stress for the type of relaxed and self-directed accomplishment that generates the Failed-Simulation Effect.

Part 3

Playbook

OF THE three laws described in this book, the law of innovation may be the most difficult to put into practice. The rules of innovation were introduced to ease the difficulty, but the many small steps required to follow these rules still inspire some tricky questions: How do I find a closed community? How do I convince them to let me enter? How do I identify the right opportunities for innovation within these communities? And so on. This playbook provides answers.

The strategies presented below roughly match the order of the innovation process as laid out in the three rules. I start with advice for identifying and entering closed communities. Among other things, I argue that you should avoid organizations with a long track record of working with high school students, and look instead to create a new position from scratch. From there, I move on to practical ways to make sure you earn your keep once inside—laying the foundation that will enable you to take advantage of opportunities for innovation as they arise. You'll learn about a mysterious-sounding (but easy-to-implement) tactic known as the *shadow job.* I'll then review one of my favorite techniques, *the inno-vation map,* which will improve your ability to turn potential innovation into real results. I conclude with an advanced strategy, known as *sloganizing,* that will help you squeeze the most impact out of your projects once they're under way.

When you combine these practical lessons with the big ideas from the preceding chapters of Part 3, you'll be armed with everything you need to wield innovation as a crucial weapon in your transformation into a relaxed superstar.

Go Where No Student Has Gone Before

"Students think they have to apply for already established posi-tions," Kate explained to me when we were discussing her path to innovation.

"For example, I had many friends sign up to be candy stripers at the hospital. But at a huge hospital, they've had lots of stu-dents work there, they have them answer the phone, they know exactly what their job will be. . . . There are so many student vol-unteers there doing the same thing, you won't be noticed."

Kate's insight is sharp. A dangerous trap for a student look-ing to innovate is entering a community that already has clear roles for volunteers. It's nearly impossible to stand out when your workday is confined to a rigid structure. To elaborate on Kate's example, most hospitals have a large student volunteer program. This option might seem appealing because it's a well-trod path including a clear application process, but as Kate noted, the hos-pital isn't going to allow you a chance to innovate. The people in charge already have a useful place for students—answering phones and running errands for nurses—and see no need to change this.

This observation is so important that I'll crystallize it into its own rule:

> Don't enter a community that has an established program for
> working with high school students.

If you're not one of the first, then your flexibility will be severely
limited. Instead, you need to identify organizations that don't
have routines in place for dealing with students. This gives you
room to innovate.

Returning to Kate's story, you'll notice that she followed her
own advice.

"I thought it was less stressful and more stimulating to do
something that hadn't been done," she explained, referring to
her work with a charter school that did not have an established
volunteer program. But how do you convince such a community
to let you on board?

"Find something that they're missing, something they need
help with, something that could really benefit them," Kate rec-
ommends. "Then offer to supply it."

That is just what Kate did when she used her experience as a
teacher's aide to become a general-purpose helper at the school,
tackling many of the small chores that can make teachers' lives
harder.

To enter a closed community with no established volunteer
program, follow Kate's example and point out a real need that
you can meet. Don't ask if they would allow you to volunteer for
your own benefit; the focus should be on making their lives better, not the other way around.

To improve your understanding of this strategy, I'll tell you the
story of a student named Steve, who currently attends Columbia
University. In high school, while attending a Model Congress
conference, Steve met a young woman who was involved with

an advocacy group called SustainUS. This organization focused on demonstrating that American youth were serious about environmental sustainability.

SustainUS matched the definition of a closed community. Furthermore, it was run by college students and had no formal system for including younger members. These two factors made it a perfect target for innovation, and Steve just had to figure out a way to get in. First he identified a need, and then he offered to fill it. The organization had just launched a large campaign to gather signatures of American youth in support of sustainability, with the plan of delivering them in person at an upcoming international climate conference in Johannesburg, South Africa. Steve noticed that the group needed press coverage.

"I like speaking with people, and I like writing, so media relations seemed like a natural thing for me to work on," Steve recalls. He told the people at SustainUS that he would be happy to spend afternoons on the phone, harassing journalists and trying to get their organization's name in the news. Not surprising, they were happy to have him join. Once on the inside, Steve paid his dues, diligently making calls and sending out press releases, eventually earning SustainUS a mention in *Time* magazine's Green Issue—a major coup. His success was rewarded by a slot on the Johannesburg trip, where he got to present the petition and lobby the international delegates. By the time Steve applied to college, his application was a standout.

Steve's story is a perfect illustration of this chapter's advice. He found a closed community without an existing high school volunteer program. Instead of asking the people there if they would help *him* by letting him volunteer, he pointed out specific ways he would help *them*. This gained him access, at which point the other rules of innovation—paying dues, leveraging successes—came into play.

Create a Shadow Job

Once you land a position in a closed community, you're still a long way from head-turning innovation. You must first pay your dues to open up opportunities, and this can sometimes be more difficult than you expect. Imagine that you're Steve. Once he carved out his new position, he actually had to do the work. Because he invented the job, however, there were no set hours during which he had to show up at an office. It was entirely up to him to structure his efforts. If you create your own position, you'll likely find yourself in a similarly unstructured situation. For a high school student, this type of work is hard: no one is forcing you to do it, so it's easy to push it off to the side.

To achieve innovation, you must tackle this problem. You have two options here. First, create your own structure. Set up a regular work schedule that puts you in the office during the same hours every week and then tell the other members of the organization to expect you during those times. This is how Kate got started. She arranged to be at the charter school, helping for an hour and a half a day, five days a week, and told the staff to count on her being there during those fixed times—no excuses. This solved the problem of her putting off work.

Steve's situation, however, proved more tricky. SustainUS didn't have a physical office, so his work was remote—conducted from the computer in his bedroom. This situation is surprisingly common for closed communities without established volunteer programs. My suggestion here is to create what I call a *shadow job*. The idea is simple: Pick a location outside of your house—I suggest the local library or perhaps an empty desk at your parents' office (assuming such a thing is possible). Create a schedule for your shadow job. During the hours you've designated for work, go to your quiet location and do work relating to your position in the closed community. In effect, you've created a pseudojob that *shadows* your position with your volunteer organization. The key is to make your shadow job a nonnegotiable habit—you work during your work hours, as in a real job, regardless of what else is going on. The easiest way to accomplish this is to announce your schedule to your parents, empowering them to guilt you back into line when you feel tempted to stray. I know, this goes against every teenage instinct—but it works. Sometimes you have to sacrifice a little for the health of your college application.

My final word of warning is to avoid becoming overly ambitious with this planning. You can always add extra time when it's needed, but if your *nonnegotiable* hours are too demanding, the chance that you'll violate your schedule increases. From my experience, five to ten hours of fixed work per week, without exception, is often more than enough to impress members of an organization with your diligence. And once they're impressed, opportunities for innovation will come your way.

Master the Art of Innovation Mapping

Nora Ephron, the acclaimed film director and writer, once gave an unexpected piece of advice to aspiring screenwriters: "Become a journalist first." Her logic is simple: if you don't first learn about the world and how it works, you'll end up writing yet another dumb "screenplay about your experience at summer camp."

The same argument holds true for innovation. Without exposure to other innovators, it can be difficult to come up with your own sparkling idea. Joining a closed community and paying your dues will expose you to opportunities. But if you have only limited exposure to innovation, you might still have a hard time identifying the *best* opportunities—eventually defaulting to the extracurricular equivalent of writing a screenplay about summer camp.

Consider this e-mail I received in late December 2008. It was sent by a student named Larry, and it began: "I feel pushed to do something that will make me stand out." He had recently read my blog post on the Failed-Simulation Effect, and though he understood the concept, he had a hard time translating it into practice.

"Innovation is not easy," he said. "I'm having trouble starting a project. I feel like almost all ideas are out of reach."

As I questioned Larry, it turned out that he was well positioned for innovation. At the time, he was working on an application for a scholarship that funds high school students' ideas for helping the world. All he had to do was propose something innovative—the most interesting ideas would win the money. But Larry couldn't see beyond the proverbial screenplay about summer camp.

"The contest wants an amazing, original, ingenious idea. I can't think of any right now," he concluded morosely.

I don't blame Larry for his lack of an "amazing, original, ingenious idea" The problem is not a shortage of creativity; it's a shortage of experience with innovation. After an extended period of brainstorming, the best idea Larry could come up with was using the scholarship money to help raise even more money to give away to a good cause—hardly a daring concept. What he needed was more exposure to what innovative ideas look like and how they get started.

In this section, I'll help you gain the experience that Larry lacks. At the core of my method is *the innovation map*—a simple technique to bolster your innovation expertise. My goal is to prepare you to see the *right* opportunities when you arrive at a situation where it's up to you to figure out what to do next. I don't want you to end up blinded, like Larry, to the vast array of fascinating projects waiting out there to be discovered.

At a high level, the innovation map work as follows. You identify a young person who has done something unquestionably impressive. If possible, you focus on an accomplishment that overlaps a field that interests you. Then you deconstruct the young person's path from average kid to innovative superstar. This deconstruction is represented as a map with arrows connecting accomplishments in chronological order. Each accomplishment is labeled with two things: the precipitating event or action that *made it possible* and the work *required to complete it*. Such a map can provide a deep understanding of exactly how an accomplishment came to be. It's an exercise in demystification. If you become adept at this technique, you'll begin to see possibilities in your own life that you never would have imagined before

Let's build an example map. Because Kate has served us so well throughout this playbook, I will once again turn to her story. Below is an innovation map that captures her rise to stardom. (For simplicity, I'll focus just on the research that changed the school's teaching methods. The starting of the Varsity Study Teams could be described in a similar map.)

Precipitating Event	Her dad suggested it to her.
Accomplishment	She became a teacher's aide.
Work Required	She had to show up at set hours each week and be useful to the teacher.

$$\downarrow$$

Precipitating Event	The teacher she was helping took a job at a charter school. The two came up with the independent study proposal as a way to allow Kate to continue to help the teacher.
Accomplishment	Kate set up an independent study project to work at a nearby charter school.

Work Required	She worked with the teacher to put together a proposal that would be approved by the school.

↓

Precipitating Event	Kate became "part of the family" at the new charter school by staying well past her scheduled 1.5 hours and making herself useful to the teachers. When it came time to start the research project required by her independent study proposal, the teachers were happy to suggest ideas and help set up interviews at the other schools in their network.
Accomplishment	She did research on the reading programs at half-a-dozen schools.
Work Required	She spent time each week reading about theories of education. She also spent a week traveling to the schools and conducting teacher interviews.

↓

Precipitating Event	During her research visits, Kate came across a school where a novel reading technique was producing remarkable results.
Accomplishment	She changed the way her charter school taught reading.
Work Required	She prepared a careful presentation of her findings that helped convince the school that this new technique had merit.

Now let's see how this map helps us better understand Kate's path to innovation. When I describe Kate to the parents of high school students, their typical response is a sigh, usually followed by some variation of the following quip: "My kid has to compete with that? He's only a teenager, how is he supposed to develop a passion that strong?" The assumption is that Kate's accomplishment must have been the result of a focused effort fueled by a burning passion. That is, she woke up one morning and cried: "I'm going to change the way they teach reading in this town!"

The innovation map above refutes this assumption. It shows that Kate was not driven by single-minded focus. She had no particular interest in changing a charter school's reading program until near the end of her circuitous path, when she happened into that classroom that was using a novel technique. The idea that some long-term passion drove her to this result is erroneous. Those parents should sigh in relief, not frustration, as Kate's map reveals that their teenage son or daughter doesn't need a cause—a preference for doing interesting things should suffice.

Another typical response goes as follows: "I want my kid to do well, but I also want her to have a normal social life, not spend all of her time on some grand project to save the world." The logic here is that big accomplishments require big investments of time. These parents imagine Kate, late at night in the library, working feverishly on her brilliant plan for overhauling reading instruction.

Again, the innovation map comes to the rescue. When you isolate the elements from the "work required" field, you end up with the following:

* She had to show up in the classroom at set hours each week and do what the teacher asked.

* She had to work with the teacher to put together an
  independent study proposal that would be approved by the
  school.
* Throughout the semester, she was required to do weekly
  background reading that brought her up to speed on
  the theories. She also had to spend a week interviewing
  teachers.
* After the interviews, she had to spend a couple weeks
  putting together a careful presentation of the information
  she had gathered.

Keep in mind that these actions occurred *one after the other*, not
all at the same time. When you read this list, nothing strikes
you as particularly onerous. It instead comes across like a regular
commitment—perhaps more time-consuming than the French
club, but less time-consuming than a varsity sport. The magic
of the innovation map is that it clearly identifies the exact work
required, helping you avoid your instinct to sensationalize the
path to sensational accomplishment.

The final reaction I get from parents goes something like this:
"My kid is talented, but he's not the type of genius that can think
up ideas that will change the way major organizations operate."
When they hear about Kate, they imagine her sitting among a
collection of stumped experts, furrowing her brow, and then suddenly yelling, "Eureka!" before sharing her genius vision with the
world. The innovation map once again brings us back to reality.
If you isolate the precipitating events fields, you discover that the
path to Kate's final insight required no leaps of brilliance. In fact,
when seen by themselves, they seem almost mundane:

* She volunteered as a teacher's aide on her dad's
  suggestion.
* She proved her worth to the teacher, and this led to an

    independent study project so she could continue to help at
    the teacher's new school.

* She become "part of the family" at the charter school by
staying well past her scheduled 1.5 hours in the afternoon,
getting to know the teachers, and being helpful. When it
came time to start work on her required research project,
they helped set up interesting interviews.

* During her research visits she came across a school where
a novel classroom technique was working well.

Notice that outside of making the initial decision to volunteer in the classroom, Kate didn't instigate the other opportunities on her path—she simply took advantage of them when they became available. Nowhere in the above list does Kate arrive at a particularly original or brilliant insight. Instead, a more boring pattern becomes apparent. Each time she was given an opportunity, Kate worked hard, and each bout of hard work brought about new opportunities.

These traits—jumping at opportunities and doing well—are admirable, and not every student possesses them. But they have nothing to do with being a genius capable of producing extraordinary ideas. The innovation map isolates this reality and therefore provides an accurate picture of how remarkable activities actually unfold.

If you're serious about innovation, then you should become serious about innovation maps. By describing Kate's accomplishment with this tool, I was able to construct her path and highlight the practical steps behind her progress. Imagine how good you could become at the art of innovation if you applied the same technique to a variety of standout students.

A good place to start is at your own high school. Identify a senior or a recent graduate who did something that strikes you as innovative. Send her an e-mail explaining that you attend the same school, are impressed by her accomplishment, and are hoping to find out more. Suggest a phone call. As someone who does these interviews for a living, I can assure you that 99 percent of students are flattered by such attention and will be happy to chat. When you get her on the phone, ask for a step-by-step recollection of her accomplishment. If you keep the innovation map format in mind while conducting this interview, it will guide you to the right types of questions. (For example: "How did you get that position? Where did you hear about it? What was required to apply?")

After the conversation, use your notes to build a map like the one I constructed for Kate. This forces you to identify what was required to achieve the ultimate accomplishment.

You can also move beyond your own school in search of innovative students. Whenever you encounter a young person who seems impressive—perhaps you read about his winning a scholarship in your local paper, or you saw his picture in a magazine—you can perform a debriefing. Just follow the strategy of sending an e-mail, expressing admiration, and asking if the person is willing to chat.

If you're able to build just three or four innovation maps, your perspective on accomplishment will be transformed. Whereas before you were baffled and intimidated, you'll now find a new sense of confidence and the world will suddenly seem full of possibility.

Seek Sloganable Projects

In 2008, Chris Guillebeau enjoyed a stunning rise to online prominence. In the spring of that year, he launched a blog titled The Art of Non-Conformity (http://chrisguillebeau.com/3x5/). It featured the tagline "Unconventional Strategies for Life, Work, and Travel." Although other blogs tackled similar topics, Chris's audience grew at an outstanding rate. By the spring of 2009, his blog was a hit. Chris was featured twice in the *New York Times*, was hired to write a column for the *Oregonian* newspaper, and became a regular contributor to the megasite The Huffington Post. In under a year, he was able to abandon the technology consulting business he used to pay the bills and instead support himself full-time with his growing online empire.

In a vivid illustration of Chris's newfound clout, a few weeks before I started writing this chapter, he sent me a note to cancel a planned phone conversation.

"You won't believe this," he apologized. "Air New Zealand is sending me down to the Cook Islands next week."

Later, I read his article about the experience. After I heard about the tropical lagoons, the white sand beaches, the "free cocktails and bottles of wine that kept appearing at the dinner table," and the sputtering buses on Rarotonga Island's perimeter road, it hit me how much Chris's life had transformed in a very short time. (I first met Chris right after his initial blog launch, so I've been able to observe, with excitement, his saga unfolding.)

Chris isn't a high school student, but his story still proves important to our quest to crack innovation. The principle at the core of his rapid success is relevant to anyone looking to get the most impact out of an unconventional project. To understand this principle, it helps to first review a sampling of Chris's recent media coverage.

In May 2009, the *New York Times* published an article about Chris that was titled "A Plan to See Every Country on Earth by the Age of 35." That same month, Chris contributed an article to Anderson Cooper's CNN blog; the post was titled "My Journey to Every Country on the Planet." Earlier that year, when Chris was quoted in the *Washington Times*, he was described as "an experienced jet-setter who has been to 103 countries," and his contributor biography on The Huffington Post reads: "Chris

Guillebeau is a writer, entrepreneur, and world traveler with the goal of visiting every country in the world."

Sense a pattern?

This media coverage all centers on the same remarkable fact: Chris has a goal of visiting every country in the world, and has already been to 103.* When you first meet Chris, this is the single fact that you'll definitely remember. When a reporter pitches a profile of Chris to an editor, I imagine that this is the lead the reporter proposes. When you visit Chris's blog, and you read his stories of sleeping in an abandoned monastery in the Dominican Republic (what he was up to the last time I spoke with him) or talking his way into Pakistan without a visa, you think, "This is a blog I want to keep reading."

Chris's project to visit every country is innovative. Without more details about round-the-world tickets, frequent-flier miles, the reality of hostels, sleeping on airport floors, and all the other tricks he uses to make his globe-trotting feasible, the plan to visit every country triggers the Failed-Simulation Effect. You are impressed, and because of this you stick around to hear what this impressive guy has to say.

But there's something more going on here. In addition to triggering the Failed-Simulation Effect, Chris's project has the extra bonus that it's easy to explain. In one short phrase—"I'm visiting every country in the world"—its impressiveness hits you full force, no further explanation necessary. Of equal importance, the idea is simple to pass on. If a friend were to interrupt you at this exact moment and ask what you're reading about, you'd have no problem describing Chris, and your friend would immediately understand why he was interesting and impressive.

---

* By the time I was editing this chapter, in September 2009, the count was up to 117. By the time you read this, it will undoubtedly be much higher. You can monitor it for yourself at http://chrisguillebeau.com/3x5/.

I call projects such as Chris's *sloganable* because they're crisp and easy to convey—like a good slogan. Described in more detail, a sloganable project is one that can be summarized in a pithy sentence that immediately triggers the full Failed-Simulation Effect.

Not all innovative projects are sloganable. Some require more explanation to trigger the desired effect. To highlight the difference, consider the following students and their projects.

- A student started the community service board at his high school and created an alliance with the local hospital to help supply the hospital with student volunteers from his school.
- A student wrote a bestselling book.
- A student worked in the research lab at her local college. She was involved in a project that looked at the role of a certain enzyme in a process related to cancer growth. She was included as a coauthor of the paper published on the subject.
- A student started a business that she sold for over a million dollars.

All four of these projects qualify as innovative. Most people can't simulate how a teenager could accomplish any of them. Only the second and fourth items, however, are also sloganable. Their pithy descriptions capture everything necessary to convey their impressiveness. The other two require some more explanation: the feeling of impressiveness doesn't immediately hit you full force; instead, it arises only after you've given the matter some thought.

Sloganable activities also provide two extra boosts in the admissions process. First, they transform your admissions file from a generic collection of accomplishments into something more personal. Consider Maneesh from earlier in Part 3, who actually did write a bestselling book. As his file moved through the admissions process at Stanford, the officers there likely took to thinking of him as "the kid who wrote the book." Such an association provides a huge advantage. It's hard for the officers to give up on "the kid who wrote the book" when just mentioning him triggers the full Failed-Simulation Effect. The same can't be said, however, for our young scientist example. The short description of this student might be "the kid with impressive involvement in science." Notice the difference. This phrase is a pointer to a more complicated description; it cannot, by itself, trigger the Failed-Simulation Effect. These variations are subtle, but in a competitive process that's rife with subjective evaluations, they matter. If the very mention of your file catches people's attention, you're going to do much better in the admissions process.

The second advantage of sloganable innovation plays out before your application ever arrives at an admissions office. For the same amount of effort invested, a sloganable project will grow in impressiveness faster than a nonsloganable project. Chris received lots of media attention because his project had an interesting hook. If he had spent the same amount of time on something equally innovative but harder to describe, it's unlikely that the *New York Times* would have shown up at the party. The *Times* is not going to publish something about the student working to revamp the relationship between a local hospital and his high school. But the idea of a guy trying to visit every country in the world has a nice ring to it. For another example, let's return to Maneesh. His sloganable project of writing a bestselling book quickly earned him a spot on a TV show. (This required no extra effort on his part; it came along as a reward for his book's success.) If he had devoted the same amount of time he spent writing the book to a nonsloganable but still innovative activity, he would have been unlikely to stumble into such an impressive bonus accomplishment.

These observations point to a single idea: All things being equal, when you're choosing an innovative project, the more sloganable the one you choose, the better. There's no magic procedure for making a project sloganable, but I can offer a few pieces of advice that may help transform an innovative idea into something even better:

- **Strip the idea to its core**. When students seek innovative projects, they often settle on complicated assemblages of several related ideas. The mind-set, I guess, is that more is better than less. *It's not!* Strip off the superfluous initiatives and actions and get down to a core outcome. If you can't explain it in one sentence, you need to simplify.

- **Inflate your ambition**. Once you've identified your core project, perform a simple thought experiment: What would it mean to double the ambition of this project? For example, if you were planning to set up a program with a local school, you might consider inflating your ambition to a program for the local school district, or perhaps for every school in the state. Next, ask whether this inflated version of the core project is still feasible. Often it turns out that getting a project started is harder than growing it once it's going. And the bigger the scope, the more sloganable the project becomes.

- **Apply the Jaded-Brother Test**. Finally, it's time to see if your efforts have passed into sloganable territory. Imagine that you have a jaded twin brother who is loath to give any sign that he's impressed with you. If you were to successfully complete your streamlined and ambitious project, how would he react? If even the jaded brother would have to grudgingly admit some pride, then you're in a good place. If not, consider starting with a new idea and going through these steps again.

I'll illustrate this process with a quick example. Imagine a student name Joe who talked his way into an internship with an education nonprofit. He's been paying his dues and is starting to earn the trust of his employers. As time goes on, he's learned more about how the organization functions, and is starting to see opportunities for potential innovation. Here's one of his ideas:

* "The staff here is overworked and there are lots of students, like me, who are willing to volunteer. Maybe I could organize more volunteers from my school to come help at the nonprofit. Perhaps it would be nice to have a formal summer internship program that brings in the best of these students. Maybe I could even launch a Web site that students can use to apply."

Joe has homed in on the big-picture idea that his nonprofit needs assistance and there are other student volunteers who could help. His description, however, is crowded—too many little ideas jumbled together. According to the process outlined above, his first step is to strip the idea down to its core. For Joe, this might mean reducing his idea to the following:

* "Set up a formal internship alliance between my high school and the nonprofit."

This streamlined idea is better because it's easier to understand. It's getting closer to a sloganable endeavor, but it's not quite there yet. The next step for Joe is to inflate his ambition. What changes would he have to make to transform the idea into something twice as impressive? After some thought, he comes up with the following:

★ "Set up a nonprofit-volunteer portal that connects students
   in my district to local nonprofits."

Joe realized that matching students at this school to this single
nonprofit could easily be expanded to multiple schools and multiple nonprofits—once the infrastructure is set up, it's easy to
scale.

Joe's final step is to apply the Jaded-Brother Test. This is
subjective, but most people have a good intuitive sense as to
whether a project would impress a cynical third party. Joe realizes
that his confusing initial idea might have elicited an unenthu-
siastic response: "You did a lot of little projects for that place.
Great." His final idea, however, is more inescapably impressive.
The idea of a teenager setting up a nonprofit portal immediately
triggers the Failed-Simulation Effect—no further description is
necessary. Even a jaded brother would grudgingly admit that he
was impressed. These three steps helped transform a loose collection of ideas into something sloganable. Joe has become "the student who runs the nonprofit-volunteer portal." Because of this,
his efforts will return much richer rewards.

Chris Guillebeau went through a similar thought process
when coming up with his own sloganable project. After college,
he volunteered to work in West Africa. He returned to the States
to earn a graduate degree with the goal of better understanding
the African continent. As his work toward the degree neared
completion, he began to think about what to do next. He knew
he wanted to be connected to the world—to travel and to help
people. Dozens of ideas crossed his mind. Maybe he could return
to the volunteer organization in West Africa? Maybe he could
raise funds to start his own organization? Maybe he could stay in
academia or become a journalist who wrote about such regions?
These are all interesting ideas—though none would elicit much

press coverage. At some point, however, he distilled his aspirations down to a simple idea: to travel the world and write about it. He then inflated the ambition into something truly sloganable: to visit *every country in the world* by the age of thirty-five. Chris's patience in waiting to find this perfect idea—an idea that's inescapably innovative—fueled his rapid rise.

The same will hold for you. As you begin to prove yourself in your closed community, have the patience to sift through available opportunities, waiting for that one sharp concept that can be forged into something sloganable. Don't be deterred if you end up applying the three steps of sloganable innovation again and again in search of the right idea. Once you've found your own sloganable pursuit, you'll be in for a wild ride.

Pulling It All Together

In late summer 2009 I signed up for sculling classes. For the uninitiated, sculling has you row one of those narrow boats with the sliding seats, holding an oar in each hand. To my surprise, the experience provided an interesting new perspective on innovation. When you watch an expert sculler, his motions seem effortless and beautiful. Each smooth stroke glides him across the water with only the faintest ripple of wake to mark his course. Watching an expert innovator is a similar experience. When you encounter a student, like those you met in Part 3, who seems to glide effortlessly into one awe-inspiring project after another, the effect is beautiful.

But then there's the reality of trying to follow the expert's example. My first afternoon in a rowing scull taught me an important lesson: sculling is *hard*. Here's what they don't tell you: those narrow little boats are incredibly difficult to balance. If you don't move every part of your body in perfect synchronization, you'll flop back and forth, slapping your paddles onto the water on either side like a drunken duck failing to gain flight. The expert rowers, it turns out, first mastered a large number of small physical details before they could even approximate anything graceful.

Innovation imposes a similar requirement. It's one thing to watch the expert innovators and appreciate their practiced wielding of the Failed-Simulation Effect. It's another thing altogether to emulate them. This is where this final playbook enters the scene. I taught you about identifying the right communities to join and then paying your dues once there. With innovation maps you learned how to polish the quality of your ideas, and with the subtle art of sloganizing, you saw how to squeeze an extra kick out of your innovation. Think of these as the small details you have to master before you can achieve an overall gracefulness in your actions.

As you put these techniques into practice, I want you to remember the frustration of the first-time sculler. Innovation won't come easily at first as you're struggling to master all the moves. But once the subsidiary skills click into place, it will be like achieving that perfect balanced stroke. You'll realize that your effort was, without a doubt, worth it.

Conclusion

I RESISTED writing a book about college admissions for a long time. It wasn't due to a lack of material. As my first two books became cult hits on college campuses, they began to find their way into the hands of high school students, who would then discover my blog and write me for guidance. Many of their questions concerned college admissions. Unwilling to turn away any student needing help, I applied to their issues the same investigative strategy that had worked so well for undergraduates: I found examples of students who had sidestepped the problem in question and then asked them how they did it. This quest soon led me to the relaxed superstars, and it wasn't long before I had decoded their three laws. With this information secured, I could offer strong advice to the high school students who wrote me, and then use their feedback to strengthen my understanding even more. After a while, it became clear that I had stumbled onto an entirely new approach to the college admissions process—an approach that was proving to be incredibly effective.

Even after I recognized the power of the relaxed superstar

philosophy, however, I still resisted the idea of writing a book on the topic. My reason was the emotional heat that surrounds the topic of college admissions. High school students and their parents instinctively bristle when the subject is mentioned, ranting about the underhanded tactics adopted by their classmates or shaking a fist against the arbitrary nature of the decisions. I don't blame them for this reaction. The modern admissions process has imposed an impossible strain on families. On the one hand, as much as we don't like to admit it out loud, it *does* matter where you go to college. A better institution will surround you with better peers and professors, and reputation alone can open doors shut to graduates of most other colleges. At the same time, the battle to gain acceptance at one of the better colleges can be brutal, exposing students to unhealthy amounts of stress. Parents may feel they are forced to choose between the student's future and the student's health—a gut-wrenching choice. I completely understand, therefore, why the very mention of college admissions can arouse hostility.

No single event eliminated my resistance to entering this fray. Instead, it was the steady drip of students' testimonials about their experience with my philosophy that eroded my mental barriers. The standard approach for tackling admissions stress is twofold: first, argue that there's more to life than Harvard; second, emphasize the negative effects of overwork and stress. I noticed, however, that the students who need this advice the most are also the most likely to ignore it; they have too much invested in the idea of getting into a good school to give up now. "I can make it," they think. "Just a couple more years and then I'll earn my rewards." Their parents often tacitly agree. "I know this can be rough for some students," they justify, "but my kid's different, he can get through it."

The relaxed superstar philosophy penetrates this resolve. Because it couples stress *reduction* with impressiveness *inflation*, these students were willing to hear me out. As more of them reported back about the dramatic improvements to their life (and admissions prospects) generated by the relaxed superstar approach, I realized that this advice might be their only shot at achieving a sustainable and healthy lifestyle. The realization spurred me into action. It was time to add a new voice to the college admissions conversation—one that avoids demonizing ambition yet still aims to reduce the negative effects such ambition can create.

I hope this book changed your thinking about this difficult process. Getting into a good college doesn't have to be a reward for extreme sacrifice; it can be, instead, a side effect of the much grander goal of building a meaningful and engaging life. As I hope my case studies have convinced you, the relaxed superstar strategy works. It will make you a better applicant at the same time that it makes you a better person. If you can muster the courage to ignore the poisonous conventional wisdom on "the art of getting in," and embrace the approach outlined in the pages you've just read, stress-free college admissions can become a reality of your student life.

References

Chapter 2

Linda Caldwell, Cheryl Baldwin, Theodore Walls, and Ed Smith. "Preliminary Effects of a Leisure Education Program to Promote Healthy Use of Free Time among Middle School Adolescents." *Journal of Leisure Research* 36.3 (2004): 310–335.

Shari Melman, Steven G. Little, and K. Angeleque Akin-Little. "Adolescent Overscheduling: The Relationship Between Levels of Participation in Scheduled Activities and Self-Reported Clinical Symptomology." *The High School Journal* 90.3 (2007): 18–30.

Chapter 7

Sherwin Rosen. "The Economics of Superstars." *The American Economic Review* 71.5 (1981): 845–858.

Chapter 8

Robert K. Merton. "The Matthew Effect in Science: The Reward and Communication Systems of Science Are Considered." *Science* 159.3810 (1968): 56–63.

Chapter 9

Nick Feltovich, Rich Harbaugh, and Ted To. "Too Cool for School? Signalling and Countersignalling." *RAND Journal of Economics* 33 (2002): 630–649.

Chapter 12

Mark D. Alicke, Frank M. LoSchiavo, Jennifer Zerbst, and Sha-obo Zhang. "The Person Who Outperforms Me Is a Genius: Maintaining Perceived Competence in Upward Social Comparison." *Journal of Personality and Social Psychology* 73.4 (1997): 781–789.

G. Daniel Lassiter and Patrick J. Munhall. "The Genius Effect: Evidence for a Nonmotivational Interpretation." *Journal of Experimental Social Psychology* 37.4 (2001): 349–355.

Acknowledgments

MY THANKS must go first and foremost to my wife, Julie, for both her tolerance and her insight during the writing of this book. Not only does she accept my monastic writing sessions with good cheer, but her comments make my work better than I could ever achieve on my own. In the same spirit, I tip my hat to my indefatigable agent, Laurie Abkemeier, who, as always, demonstrated her uncanny ability to take my high-volume spray of esoteric ideas and extract crisp, focused topics that are understandable to normal human beings. I must also thank Becky Cole for her faith in this project, Laura Swerdloff for her help in shaping the book's structure, and, of course, my editor, Hallie Falquet, for her tireless efforts in polishing the manuscript into something special.

Finally, it's hard to fully express my gratitude to the dozens of relaxed superstars who took the time to answer my endless questions. I'm inspired by their willingness to help other students find stress-free paths through high school and the college admissions process, and I can only hope that this book lives up to their expectations.

About the Author

Cal Newport graduated from Dartmouth College, earned a Ph.D. from MIT, and is now an associate professor of computer science at Georgetown University. The author of multiple bestselling books, he runs the popular blog *Study Hacks*, which explores the impact of technology on our ability to perform productive work and lead satisfying lives. His contrarian ideas have been featured on many major media platforms, including the *New York Times*, *Wall Street Journal*, *Washington Post*, *The Economist*, and NPR. Visit him online at calnewport.com.

Don't miss Cal Newport's other popular student success guides.